Troubleshooting OpenStack

Get unstuck and start stacking!

Tony Campbell

[PACKT] open source*
PUBLISHING   community experience distilled

BIRMINGHAM - MUMBAI

Troubleshooting OpenStack

First published: March 2016

Production reference: 1170316

Published by Packt Publishing Ltd.
Livery Place
35 Livery Street
Birmingham B3 2PB, UK.

ISBN 978-1-78398-688-0

www.packtpub.com

Credits

Author
Tony Campbell

Reviewer
Cody Bunch

Acquisition Editor
Divya Poojari

Content Development Editor
Trusha Shriyan

Technical Editor
Pranjali Mistry

Copy Editor
Neha Vyas

Project Coordinator
Kinjal Bari

Proofreader
Safis Editing

Indexer
Rekha Nair

Production Coordinator
Melwyn Dsa

Cover Work
Melwyn Dsa

About the Author

Tony Campbell grew up in the heart of Silicon Valley where he had access and exposure to many technology companies that led the Internet boom. He started programming in the early 90s and has been hooked since then. Tony is committed to helping others understand and successfully adopt OpenStack.

About the Reviewer

Cody Bunch is a private cloud/virtualization architect. He has authored and coauthored several OpenStack and VMware books. Additionally, he has been a technical editor on a number of projects. Cody also frequently speaks at industry events and in local user groups, and he runs the vSensei mentorship program as well.

He has reviewed this book as well as OpenStack Networking Essentials. He has also the following books for Packt Publishing:

VMware vCloud Director Cookbook

Managing VMware Infrastructure with Windows PowerShell

VMware VI and vSphere SDK: Managing the VMware Infrastructure and vSphere

www.PacktPub.com

eBooks, discount offers, and more

Did you know that Packt offers eBook versions of every book published, with PDF and ePub files available? You can upgrade to the eBook version at www.PacktPub.com and as a print book customer, you are entitled to a discount on the eBook copy. Get in touch with us at customercare@packtpub.com for more details.

At www.PacktPub.com, you can also read a collection of free technical articles, sign up for a range of free newsletters and receive exclusive discounts and offers on Packt books and eBooks.

https://www2.packtpub.com/books/subscription/packtlib

Do you need instant solutions to your IT questions? PacktLib is Packt's online digital book library. Here, you can search, access, and read Packt's entire library of books.

Why subscribe?

- Fully searchable across every book published by Packt
- Copy and paste, print, and bookmark content
- On demand and accessible via a web browser

This book is dedicated in the loving memory of my mother, Joyce E. Campbell, who was the first to ignite my passion for technology.

Table of Contents

Preface

OpenStack is one of the fastest growing open source projects in the history. Its rapid adoption and popularity has led to an increase in the demand of OpenStack talent. The skills you will learn in this book will help you position yourself as an effective OpenStack troubleshooter.

What this book covers

Chapter 1, *The Troubleshooting Toolkit*, covers various tools that will provide invaluable as you troubleshoot OpenStack.

Chapter 2, *Troubleshooting OpenStack Identity*, helps you to quickly recognize and resolve identity and authentication issues.

Chapter 3, *Troubleshooting the OpenStack Image Service*, fixes problems with Glance, the OpenStack Image service.

Chapter 4, *Troubleshooting OpenStack Networking*, shows you how to resolve networking problems within your OpenStack cluster.

Chapter 5, *Troubleshooting OpenStack Compute*, adverts that the compute service is central to OpenStack, and this chapter includes helpful tips for quickly getting things resolved in case the service breaks.

Chapter 6, *Troubleshooting OpenStack Block Storage*, explores ways to resolve issues with persistent storage in an OpenStack cluster.

Chapter 7, *Troubleshooting OpenStack Object Storage*, introduces you to object storage in OpenStack and helps you master the techniques to resolve common issues.

Chapter 8, *Troubleshooting the OpenStack Orchestration Service*, discusses Heat, the OpenStack Orchestration service, and how to navigate through errors or problems with this service.

Chapter 9, Troubleshooting the OpenStack Telemetry Service, explores Ceilometer and how to troubleshoot issues with the telemetry processes and meters.

Chapter 10, OpenStack Performance, Availability, and Reliability, provides you with tips for maintaining the overall health of your OpenStack cluster.

What you need for this book

This book is based upon the Liberty release of OpenStack running on the Ubuntu operating system. While most of the content will be relevant to other versions of OpenStack, and alternate operating systems, the examples are based on the author's configuration.

Who this book is for

You will need a basic understanding of OpenStack, Linux, and cloud computing. If you have an understanding of Linux, this book will help you leverage that knowledge in the world of OpenStack, giving you confidence to tackle most issues that may arise.

Conventions

In this book, you will find a number of text styles that distinguish between different kinds of information. Here are some examples of these styles and an explanation of their meaning.

Code words in text, database table names, folder names, filenames, file extensions, pathnames, dummy URLs, user input, and Twitter handles are shown as follows: "Typing `ceilometer help` in the terminal will give you a list of the available commands."

A block of code is set as follows:

```
instance_usage_audit = True
instance_usage_audit_period = hour
notify_on_state_change = vm_and_task_state
notification_driver = messagingv2
```

Any command-line input or output is written as follows:

```
sudo -u ceilometer ceilometer-api --config-file=/etc/ceilometer/
ceilometer.conf --log-file=/var/log/ceilometer/ceilometer-api.log
```

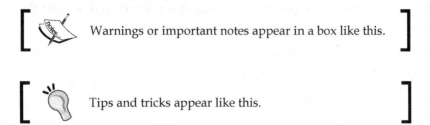

Warnings or important notes appear in a box like this.

Tips and tricks appear like this.

Reader feedback

Feedback from our readers is always welcome. Let us know what you think about this book—what you liked or disliked. Reader feedback is important for us as it helps us develop titles that you will really get the most out of.

To send us general feedback, simply e-mail feedback@packtpub.com, and mention the book's title in the subject of your message.

If there is a topic that you have expertise in and you are interested in either writing or contributing to a book, see our author guide at www.packtpub.com/authors.

Customer support

Now that you are the proud owner of a Packt book, we have a number of things to help you to get the most from your purchase.

Downloading the example code

You can download the example code files for this book from your account at http://www.packtpub.com. If you purchased this book elsewhere, you can visit http://www.packtpub.com/support and register to have the files e-mailed directly to you.

You can download the code files by following these steps:

1. Log in or register to our website using your e-mail address and password.
2. Hover the mouse pointer on the **SUPPORT** tab at the top.
3. Click on **Code Downloads & Errata**.
4. Enter the name of the book in the **Search** box.
5. Select the book for which you're looking to download the code files.
6. Choose from the drop-down menu where you purchased this book from.
7. Click on **Code Download**.

Once the file is downloaded, please make sure that you unzip or extract the folder using the latest version of:

- WinRAR / 7-Zip for Windows
- Zipeg / iZip / UnRarX for Mac
- 7-Zip / PeaZip for Linux

Errata

Although we have taken every care to ensure the accuracy of our content, mistakes do happen. If you find a mistake in one of our books—maybe a mistake in the text or the code—we would be grateful if you could report this to us. By doing so, you can save other readers from frustration and help us improve s mvvmbvubsequent versions of this book. If you find any errata, please report them by visiting http://www.packtpub.com/submit-errata, selecting your book, clicking on the **Errata Submission Form** link, and entering the details of your errata. Once your errata are verified, your submission will be accepted and the errata will be uploaded to our website or added to any list of existing errata under the Errata section of that title.

To view the previously submitted errata, go to https://www.packtpub.com/books/content/support and enter the name of the book in the search field. The required information will appear under the **Errata** section.

Piracy

Piracy of copyrighted material on the Internet is an ongoing problem across all media. At Packt, we take the protection of our copyright and licenses very seriously. If you come across any illegal copies of our works in any form on the Internet, please provide us with the location address or website name immediately so that we can pursue a remedy.

Please contact us at copyright@packtpub.com with a link to the suspected pirated material.

We appreciate your help in protecting our authors and our ability to bring you valuable content.

Questions

If you have a problem with any aspect of this book, you can contact us at questions@packtpub.com, and we will do our best to address the problem.

1
The Troubleshooting Toolkit

OpenStack is one of the fastest growing open source projects in history. It is rapidly becoming the standard for open source, public and private clouds. Since its first release in 2010, there have been 12 major releases, with the thirteenth being planned as of the writing of this book. The project has grown from a few thousand lines of code written by dozens of developers to over 2.6 million lines of code from over 2,100 contributors. OpenStack originally started with two projects, Object Storage (Swift) and Compute (Nova). OpenStack has grown to include over 40 projects. This huge amount of commitment and contribution has led to the momentum that OpenStack enjoys today.

OpenStack has become very popular among companies and organizations because it allows them to provide public and private clouds to their employees, partners, customers, and constituents. In addition, the vibrant community around OpenStack allows its adopters to avoid lock in and gives them freedom to work with the technologies of their choice. As an open source project, those who adopt it have the freedom to work with the community and add functionalities and features as they see fit. This flexibility has enticed hundreds of organizations to join this community, many dedicating developers to the cause.

OpenStack is extremely powerful, but it is not without complexity. One of the side effects of its rapid growth and large community involvement is the fact that things often change quickly. New projects are added regularly, and along with those projects, come new functionalities. As the community finds better ways to implement things, it often necessitates change. As the projects begin to get more and more integrated, it becomes very important to understand how these projects flow and interrelate. While the growth of OpenStack has been rapid, the development of OpenStack talent has not kept pace. As a result, individuals with OpenStack skills are in high demand.

OpenStack requires operators with the ability to identify, isolate, and troubleshoot errors that might arise in the environment. Troubleshooting OpenStack is not always straightforward because the functionality of an OpenStack cloud is delivered by several different projects all working together under the OpenStack umbrella. In addition, the OpenStack projects are further augmented by external open source technologies. With OpenStack's power and flexibility comes the challenge of pinpointing the source of errors and problems. While this challenge is real, it is by no means insurmountable.

In this book, we will show you how to find success with OpenStack troubleshooting. We will introduce you to inside tips and a winning methodology to troubleshoot your OpenStack cluster. It is assumed that you are familiar with the basic Linux administration, cloud computing in general, and OpenStack in particular. We will walk you through a set of useful tools to troubleshoot OpenStack, and we will provide a step-by-step guide to address common problems in installation, performance, availability, and automation. We will focus on central OpenStack projects, including those providing compute, storage, and networking. By the time we reach the end of this book, you will be better prepared to tackle the OpenStack troubleshooting challenges that may come your way. You will have a better understanding of how OpenStack works under the hood, and this understanding, along with the tips and methodologies presented in this book, will make you an efficient and confident OpenStack troubleshooter.

In this chapter, we will cover the following topics:

- The project overview of OpenStack
- Basic troubleshooting methods and tools
- Installing packages

The project overview of OpenStack

The more you understand about OpenStack, how it is organized and architected, the more successful you will be at troubleshooting it. In this section, we provide you with a strong foundation of understanding about OpenStack. Throughout the book, we will build on this foundation, going deeper into each project as we encounter them in future chapters. To start the journey, we will introduce you to some of the projects that are commonly deployed in an OpenStack cluster. It's worth pointing out that we won't cover every OpenStack project, but we will attempt to adequately cover each of the commonly deployed projects.

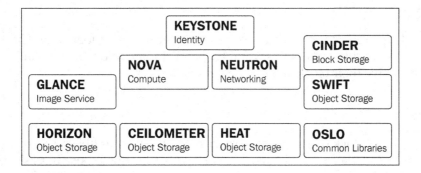

Keystone

Keystone is the OpenStack Identity service. It is responsible for authentication and is involved in authorization for an OpenStack cluster. Keystone is also responsible for service discovery, allowing users to see which services are available in a cluster. A user-initiated request will typically flow through Keystone; so, learning to troubleshoot this service is a wise investment.

Glance

Glance is the OpenStack Image service. Glance is primarily responsible for image registration and storage. As an example, compute instances can be created based on machine images. These images are typically stored through and retrieved via Glance.

Neutron

Neutron is the OpenStack Networking service. Networking is hard, and it is no different in OpenStack. Neutron is responsible for abstracting the network-related functionality in OpenStack. This is an area where many operators may run into trouble. Learning how to skillfully troubleshoot Neutron will serve you well as an OpenStack administrator.

Nova

Nova is the OpenStack Compute service. Nova provides compute instances in an OpenStack cloud. This is one of the largest OpenStack projects and one of the oldest. Nova is used heavily in an OpenStack cloud, and it is critical that troubleshooters understand this project, its concepts, components, and architecture.

Cinder

Cinder is the project that provides block storage services for OpenStack. Cinder abstracts and provides access to several backend storage options. Compute instances will often receive their block storage via the Cinder service.

Swift

Swift is the OpenStack Object Storage service. Swift provides object-based storage, which is accessed via an API. Unlike Cinder, Swift does not expose block-level storage, but it does offer a system that allows you to store petabytes of data on a cluster that is built on commodity hardware.

Heat

The OpenStack Orchestration service is named Heat. Heat allows users to leverage a declarative template language to describe, build, and deploy OpenStack resources. It is designed to allow users to manage the entire life cycle of their cloud resources.

Ceilometer

Ceilometer is the OpenStack Telemetry service, and it is responsible for collecting utilization measurements from physical and virtual resources in an OpenStack cloud.

Horizon

The OpenStack dashboard is named Horizon. Horizon provides the graphical user interface for OpenStack. It relies on the OpenStack APIs to present much of this functionality. It is an extremely useful tool when troubleshooting the APIs or OpenStack functionality in general.

Oslo

Oslo is the OpenStack project that contains the shared Python libraries that are leveraged across all projects. Examples of these include code that supports messaging, command-line programs, configuration, and logging.

Documentation

One of the strengths of the OpenStack community is that it treats documentation as a first-class citizen. In the community, documentation is just as important as code. The documentation project is structured like the others and receives a good amount of exposure and attention.

In addition to the these projects, there are several other popular projects worth mentioning. These projects include the following:

Ironic

While Nova typically handles the provisioning of virtual machines, with Ironic, users can provision physical hardware in a *cloudy* way. The Ironic driver allows you to deploy bare metal hardware in a similar fashion to the way you deploy virtual machines.

Magnum

Magnum is a project designed to allow users to manage application containers in OpenStack. This allows container orchestration engines, such as Docker and Kubernetes, to be leveraged through OpenStack.

Trove

Trove is an OpenStack service that provides cloud databases. The Trove service supports the provisioning of both relational and non-relational databases.

Barbican

Barbican is a service that facilitates the management, provisioning, and storage of secrets. Secrets include things such as passwords, encryption keys, and certificates.

Congress

Congress provides a policy as a service for OpenStack. The aim of the project is to provide a framework for regulatory compliance and governance across cloud services. Its responsibility is policy enforcement.

Designate

Designate provides DNS as a service. This service provides zone and record management as well as support for multiple nameservers.

These are just some of the many projects under the Big Tent of OpenStack. New projects with the promise of a new functionality are created regularly. As these projects gain more and more adoption, the chance that you will need to troubleshoot them increases.

The supporting technologies

One of the design tenants of OpenStack, since its inception, is to not reinvent the wheel. In other words, when a solid technology existed that met the needs of the project, the original developers would leverage the existing technology as opposed to creating their own version. The result is that OpenStack is built upon many technologies that administrators already know and love. The tools used to troubleshoot these technologies can also be used to troubleshoot OpenStack. In this section, we will go over a few of the supporting technologies that are commonly used across OpenStack projects. Where different projects use specific supporting technologies, they will be covered in the respective chapters for those projects.

Linux

The OpenStack software runs on Linux. The primary OpenStack services are Linux services. Rest-assured that all your experience in troubleshooting the Linux operating systems will serve you well in the world of OpenStack. You will come across OpenStack clusters running on just about every Linux distribution. Some deployments will leverage Linux networking, and experience in this area is extremely valuable in OpenStack. Many of the most popular Linux distributions offer packages to deploy OpenStack. Operators may optionally deploy from source or leverage one of the installers available in the market. Either way, Linux is critical to any OpenStack deployment, and we will make use of many common Linux tools when troubleshooting.

Databases

Most OpenStack services are backed by a database. The Oslo project in OpenStack provides common Python code for OpenStack projects that need to access a database. Oslo provides libraries to connect to a Postgres or MySQL database. Experience with these database engines, and others like them, is very useful when troubleshooting. As you understand the different projects and what they store in the database, you can trace a request to ensure that the state recorded in the database matches the state reported elsewhere.

Message queue

OpenStack often leverages a message broker to facilitate communication between its components. To avoid tight coupling, most components do not communicate directly with one another, but instead communication is routed through a message broker. With the message broker playing a central role in component communication, it is a powerful resource for the troubleshooter. It is possible to trace messages from one component to another and spot messages that may not be generated or delivered. This information can help lead you down the right path when attempting to isolate an issue.

The Apache web server

OpenStack projects have begun to use **Web Server Gate Interface** (**WSGI**) servers to deploy their APIs. The Apache web server is a popular choice to handle these WSGI applications. Apache troubleshooting tools and techniques are directly transferable when working with OpenStack.

Basic troubleshooting methodology and tools

There are many paths an OpenStack troubleshooter can follow when attempting to resolve an issue. It is worth arguing that there is more than one way to approach any troubleshooting problem. Operators and administrators will need to find a methodology that works well for them and the context in which they operate. With this in mind, I would like to share a methodology that I have found useful when working with OpenStack, specifically the following methodologies:

*   **Services**: Confirm that the required services are up and running.
*   **Authentication**: Ensure that authentication is properly configured.
*   **CLI Debug**: Run the CLI commands in the debug mode, looking for errors.

- Execute the request against the API directly, looking for issues.
- **Check Logs:** Check log files for traces or errors.

I have found that working through these steps when troubleshooting OpenStack will yield useful clues that will help identify, isolate, and resolve issues.

There are many tools available when troubleshooting OpenStack. In the following sections, we will cover a few of the tools that we leverage frequently. I would recommend that you add these to your toolbox if you are not already using them.

General Linux tools

OpenStack is deployed in a Linux environment; therefore, administrators can leverage popular Linux tools when troubleshooting. If you are an experienced Linux administrator, you should be comfortable with most of these tools, and you should find that your existing Linux experience will serve you well as you troubleshoot OpenStack. In this section, we will walk you through some of the more common tools that are used. We will explain how each tool can be leveraged in an OpenStack environment specifically, but if you are interested in learning how the tools work generally, much can be learned by researching each tool on the Internet.

Linux processes

OpenStack runs several processes that are critical to its smooth operation. Understanding each process can be very helpful to quickly identify and resolve problems in your cluster. It is not uncommon for the source of your problems to be rooted in the fact that a process has died or not started successfully. Bringing your cluster back to health may be as simple as restarting the necessary process. As we tackle each OpenStack project, we will introduce you to the key processes for that project's service. Like any Linux process, there are several commands that we can leverage to check these processes. Some of the common commands that we will leverage are detailed in the following sections.

ps

Hopefully, the ps command is already familiar to you as a Linux administrator. We leverage this command in OpenStack to get a snapshot of the current processes running on our host machines. The command will quickly allow us to see which OpenStack processes are running, and more importantly when troubleshooting, which OpenStack processes are not running.

We typically use the `ps` command with the standard `-aux` options and then pipe that to `grep` in order to find the OpenStack process we are interested in:

```
root@ost-controller:~# ps -aux | grep nova-
root         664  0.0  0.2 139180  8500 ?        Ssl  14:36   0:00 /usr/sbin
/nova-agent -q -p /var/run/nova-agent.pid -o /var/log/nova-agent.log -l de
bug /usr/share/nova-agent/nova-agent.py
nova       11698  0.6  2.5 281696 96804 ?        Ss   15:58   0:02 /usr/bin/
python /usr/local/bin/nova-cert --config-file=/etc/nova/nova.conf
nova       11726  0.6  1.9 244812 74200 ?        Ss   15:58   0:01 /usr/bin/
python /usr/local/bin/nova-consoleauth --config-file=/etc/nova/nova.conf
nova       11759  1.0  1.7 154468 66572 ?        Ss   15:58   0:03 /usr/bin/
python /usr/local/bin/nova-conductor --config-file=/etc/nova/nova.conf
nova       11793  0.6  1.9 246512 74236 ?        Ss   15:58   0:02 /usr/bin/
python /usr/local/bin/nova-scheduler --config-file=/etc/nova/nova.conf
nova       11843  1.8  1.9 249292 74996 ?        S    15:58   0:05 /usr/bin/
python /usr/local/bin/nova-conductor --config-file=/etc/nova/nova.conf
nova       11844  1.8  1.9 248676 74160 ?        S    15:58   0:05 /usr/bin/
python /usr/local/bin/nova-conductor --config-file=/etc/nova/nova.conf
nova       28304  3.8  2.9 1443964 113576 ?      Ssl  16:01   0:04 /usr/bin/
python /usr/local/bin/nova-compute --config-file=/etc/nova/nova.conf --con
fig-file=/etc/nova/nova-compute.conf
root       28852  0.0  0.0 11984   912 pts/0     S+   16:03   0:00 grep nova
-
```

For example, the preceding code would list each of the OpenStack Nova processes, which, by convention, are prefixed with `nova-`. It's also worth pointing out that this command may also reveal the `-log-` file option set when the process was launched. This will give you the location of the log files for each process, which will be extremely valuable during our troubleshooting.

pgrep

In addition to the `ps` command that is used to look at processes, you can also leverage the `pgrep` command. This command allows you to look up processes based on a pattern. For example, you can list processes based on their names:

```
[root@ost-controller:~# pgrep -l nova
664 nova-agent
11698 nova-cert
11726 nova-consoleaut
11759 nova-conductor
11793 nova-scheduler
11843 nova-conductor
11844 nova-conductor
28304 nova-compute
```

This command will list all the processes that have `nova` in their name. Without the `-l` option, the command would only list the process ID. If we want to see the process name too, we simply add `-l`. If you'd like to see the full-line output like we saw with `ps`, then you can add the `-a` option. With this option, you will be able to see extra attributes that are used when starting the process, including log file locations.

pkill

Along with the `pgrep` command, there is the `pkill` command. This command allows you to kill processes that match the name pattern that you provide. Take a look at the following as an example:

```
[root@ost-controller:~# pkill 28304
```

The preceding command would kill the process with `PID 20069`. This can be useful in situations where you have process hanging and you need to restart them. This is an alternative to the standard `kill` command.

top and htop

While `ps` and `pgrep` provide us with a snapshot of the running processes, `top` and `htop` will give us an interactive view of our processes. The `top` and `htop` commands are very similar, but `htop` provides you with a little added interface sugar, including the ability to scroll data. You may need to install `htop` on your servers if you decide to use it. Using either of these commands, you will be able to see the processes interactively sorted by things, such as percentage of CPU used by the process or percentage of memory. If you find your cluster in a situation where there is resource contention on the host, this tool can begin to give you an idea of which process to focus on first. The following screenshot is a sample output from `htop`:

```
  1  [|||||                        ]     Tasks: 88, 222 thr; 2 running
  2  [||||||                       ]     Load average:      0.17 0.23
  Mem[||||||||||||||||2357/3760MB]      Uptime: 02:40:29
  Swp[                             ]

  PID USER      PRI  NI  VIRT   RES   SHR S CPU% MEM%   TIME+  Command
 1732 neutron    20   0  248M 77296  2752 S  2.6  2.0  1:29.87 /usr/bin/py
 4787            20   0  129M 48908  4772 S  2.0  1.3  2:10.58 /usr/bin/py
 1734            20   0  249M 77808  2644 S  2.0  2.0  1:34.54 /usr/bin/py
 1735            20   0  241M 70200  2616 S  2.0  1.8  1:29.07 /usr/bin/py
 4815            20   0  128M 47968  4784 S  2.0  1.2  1:34.62 /usr/bin/py
 4880            20   0  128M 47856  4756 S  2.0  1.2  1:35.32 /usr/bin/py
 4919            20   0  125M 45104  4764 S  2.0  1.2  1:35.23 /usr/bin/py
11844            20   0  247M 79020  3612 S  2.0  2.1  1:30.03 /usr/bin/py
28304            20   0  141M  111M  7976 S  2.0  3.0  1:31.32 /usr/bin/py
14731 root       20   0 26256  2336  1432 R  1.3  0.1  0:00.06 htop
```

Hard drives

It's likely you will need to troubleshoot an issue that is related to hard drives when dealing with OpenStack. You can leverage standard Linux tools to interrogate the hard drive and assist you in troubleshooting.

df

There will be several moments in our OpenStack journey where we will be concerned about storage and the hard drives in our cluster that provide some of that storage. The df command will be leveraged to report on the disk space used by our filesystem. We can add the -h option to make the values human readable:

```
root@ost-controller:~# df -h
Filesystem      Size  Used Avail Use% Mounted on
udev            1.9G  8.0K  1.9G   1% /dev
tmpfs           377M  436K  376M   1% /run
/dev/xvda1       50G  4.0G   43G   9% /
none            4.0K     0  4.0K   0% /sys/fs/cgroup
none            5.0M     0  5.0M   0% /run/lock
none            1.9G     0  1.9G   0% /run/shm
none            100M     0  100M   0% /run/user
```

The output from this command tells us which filesystems are currently mounted and provides usage information for each, such as the size of the filesystem, the amount used, and the amount available. The command also tells us the mount point for each filesystem.

fdisk

In addition to df, we will leverage fdisk. The fdisk command allows us to work with the disk partition tables. This may become necessary when troubleshooting OpenStack Block Storage or working with images in OpenStack. Take the following code as an example:

```
root@ost-controller:~# fdisk -l

Disk /dev/xvda: 53.7 GB, 53687091200 bytes
255 heads, 63 sectors/track, 6527 cylinders, total 104857600 sectors
Units = sectors of 1 * 512 = 512 bytes
Sector size (logical/physical): 512 bytes / 512 bytes
I/O size (minimum/optimal): 512 bytes / 512 bytes
Disk identifier: 0x000da08a

   Device Boot      Start         End      Blocks   Id  System
/dev/xvda1   *        2048   104856254    52427103+  83  Linux
```

The preceding command will list the partition table. From the list, you can see the details about the disk, including its name and size. You can also see which partitions correspond to the disk. In addition to listing the partition table, you can also modify the partitions.

```
[root@ost-controller:~# fdisk /dev/xvda

[Command (m for help): m
Command action
   a   toggle a bootable flag
   b   edit bsd disklabel
   c   toggle the dos compatibility flag
   d   delete a partition
   l   list known partition types
   m   print this menu
   n   add a new partition
   o   create a new empty DOS partition table
   p   print the partition table
   q   quit without saving changes
   s   create a new empty Sun disklabel
   t   change a partition's system id
   u   change display/entry units
   v   verify the partition table
   w   write table to disk and exit
   x   extra functionality (experts only)

Command (m for help):
```

This command will allow you to change the partition table for the disk named /dev/xvda. After running this command, type m to see the menu of commands. Using this menu, you can create new partitions, delete existing ones, or change existing partitions.

parted

As we will discover later in this book, there are some use cases where you can't use fdisk. In those situations, we will look to another partitioning tool named parted. This tool also allows us to work with partitions. With parted, we can create, resize, copy, move, and delete partitions. The parted tool allows you to work with many different types of filesystems as compared to fdisk.

```
[root@ost-controller:~# parted
GNU Parted 2.3
Using /dev/xvda
Welcome to GNU Parted! Type 'help' to view a list of commands.
(parted)
```

The preceding command will start the parted tool. Once the tool starts, you can type `help` in the prompt to see a list of menu items. Some of the functionalities listed include `makefs`, to make filesystems; and `makepart`, to make a partition; or `makepartfs`, to make both at the same time.

cat /proc/partitions

It's worth noting that we can also run the following command to list the partitions:

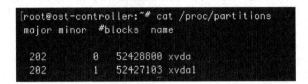

The `/proc/partitions` file is dynamic and made on the fly. Viewing this file will give you similar information as what you would find by running `fdisk -l`.

Installed packages

On Debian and Ubuntu systems, we can leverage the advanced package tool by running the `apt` command. This tool can be used to provide insight into which packages are installed on our system. This knowledge can be useful when troubleshooting OpenStack problems related to packages:

```
apt search openstack | less
```

The preceding command will list the packages that have the word `openstack` in their description and paginate the output. Running this command will give you a sense of some of the packages that come together to create an OpenStack cloud. Not all the packages listed are required, but this will give you an idea of which packages are available:

```
apt list | grep nova
```

The preceding `apt list` command will list the packages on the system. For example, we can pipe `apt list` to `grep` for `nova` to see a list of packages with nova in the name. We can take any of these packages and run them through `apt show` to get the details about the package. Take this line of command, for example:

```
apt show nova-api
```

General tools

We will make use of several Linux utilities throughout this book. Some of these tools are outlined in the following section.

The watch command

One of the many commands you may find useful when troubleshooting is the watch command. This command provides a convenient way to execute a command on a given time interval. I often use it to keep an eye on my processes when I'm trying to get them to restart. I've also leveraged this command when troubleshooting instance creation, as it allows me to check whether and when the instance becomes active:

```
watch pgrep -l nova
```

The preceding command will run the `pgrep -l nova` command every two seconds by default. You can adjust the interval at which the command is run by passing the `-n` option:

```
watch -n 3 nova list
```

This command will run the nova list command every 3 seconds.

File tools

We will leverage some commonly used Linux tools when troubleshooting. These tools include the following:

- `cat`: This is used to print files or input to the standard output.
- `less`: This is used to view files and allows you to page through those files.
- `find`: This allows you to search through files in a hierarchy of directories.
- `grep`: This allows you to search through files for lines that match a given pattern. We will use the `grep` command quite a bit as we are searching through logs for different types of messages.
- `tail`: This allows you to output the last part of a file. We will leverage the `tail` command often with the `-f` argument, which will allow us to follow a file as it is updated. This is used to watch logs live as we run different services or commands.

Message broker tools

One of the central components of any OpenStack cluster is the messaging broker. OpenStack uses a message broker to pass information back and forth between its components. The message queue facilitates intra-component communication, and as a result, it can often be a useful place to search for troubleshooting clues in an OpenStack cluster. While the default message broker installed with OpenStack is RabbitMQ, deployers have the ability to select from several other messaging technologies including ZeroMQ or QPid. We will explore some high-level troubleshooting tools for RabbitMQ in the following sections.

RabbitMQ

The RabbitMQ message system comes with a handy utility named `rabbitmqctl`. This tool allows operators to complete several useful tasks, but here we will highlight a few that are particularly helpful to troubleshoot OpenStack.

```
[root@ost-controller:~# rabbitmqctl status
Status of node 'rabbit@ost-controller' ...
[{pid,22934},
 {running_applications,[{rabbit,"RabbitMQ","3.2.4"},
                        {os_mon,"CPO  CXC 138 46","2.2.14"},
                        {mnesia,"MNESIA  CXC 138 12","4.11"},
                        {xmerl,"XML parser","1.3.5"},
                        {sasl,"SASL  CXC 138 11","2.3.4"},
                        {stdlib,"ERTS  CXC 138 10","1.19.4"},
                        {kernel,"ERTS  CXC 138 10","2.16.4"}]},
```

The preceding command will return the status of your RabbitMQ message broker. It can be helpful to check the output of this command for any errors. For example, if you see an error that starts with `Error: unable to connect to node`, then this means that RabbitMQ is likely not running. You can run the following command on Ubuntu to try and start it:

```
sudo service rabbitmq-server start
```

```
rabbitmqctl stop
```

The preceding command will stop your RabbitMQ message broker. You can use the same service command from the one we used here to restart it.

```
root@ost-controller:~# rabbitmqctl list_queues
Listing queues ...
cert    0
cert.ost-controller     0
cert_fanout_ac5d6a128b0849b79153c43ffd7ed417     0
compute 0
compute.ost-controller  0
```

The list_queues command will list the queues in your message broker. When you run this on an OpenStack cluster, you will be able to see the decent number of queues used by the software to pass messages back and forth between OpenStack components. In addition to the name of the queues, this command can show you several attributes for each queue. Select the attributes you want to see by passing them after your list_queues command.

```
root@ost-controller:~# rabbitmqctl list_queues name durable messages_ready
 consumers
Listing queues ...
cert    false   0       1
cert.ost-controller     false   0       1
cert_fanout_ac5d6a128b0849b79153c43ffd7ed417    false   0       1
compute false   0       1
compute.ost-controller  false   0       1
```

In this command, we are requesting several columns of data directly after the list_queues command. Running the command this way will return a tab-delimited list including the name of the queue, whether or not the queue is durable, the number of messages ready to be read from the queue, the number of consumers listening to the queue, and the current queue state.

```
root@ost-controller:~# rabbitmqctl list_exchanges
Listing exchanges ...
        direct
amq.direct      direct
amq.fanout      fanout
amq.headers     headers
amq.match       headers
amq.rabbitmq.log        topic
amq.rabbitmq.trace      topic
amq.topic       topic
ceilometer      topic
```

Like the `list_queues` command, there is also a `list_exchanges` command, which allows you to see the exchanges in your message broker. Running this command on an OpenStack cluster will allow you to see the exchanges that OpenStack leverages. Exchanges sit between message producers and the queues where those messages will eventually reside. The exchange is responsible for taking the message from the message producer and delivering that message to the appropriate queue if there is any queue at all:

```
rabbitmqctl list_exchanges name type durable policy
```

Running the `list_exchanges` command with the name, type, durable, and policy column headers, as demonstrated in the preceding line of code, will output the exchanges and their respective values for each column. Specifically, the name of the exchange; the exchange type which is either direct, topic, headers, or fanout; whether or not the exchange is durable, meaning it will survive a server restart; and finally, the exchange's policy. Policies are a method by which administrators can control the behavior of queues and exchanges across the entire RabbitMQ cluster. You can see which policies, if any, are configured by running this:

```
rabbitmqctl list_policies
```

In RabbitMQ, exchanges are related to queues through bindings. Queues use bindings to tell exchanges that they are interested in messages flowing through that exchange. You can list the bindings by running this code:

```
[root@ost-controller:~# rabbitmqctl list_bindings
Listing bindings ...
        exchange        cert    queue   cert    []
        exchange        cert.ost-controller     queue   cert.ost-controlle
r       []
        exchange        cert_fanout_ac5d6a128b0849b79153c43ffd7ed417      qu
eue     cert_fanout_ac5d6a128b0849b79153c43ffd7ed417    []
        exchange        compute queue   compute []
        exchange        compute.ost-controller  queue   compute.ost-contro
ller    []
```

The `list bindings` command will display each of the bindings between exchanges and queues. By default, it will list the name of the source, the type of the source, the name of the destination, the type of the destination, a routing key, and any binding arguments.

To view a list of RabbitMQ clients with connections to the RabbitMQ server, run the `list_connections` command:

```
rabbitmqctl list_connections
```

This command will list the username associated with the connection, the hostname of the connected peer, the port of the peer, and the state of the connection.

Summary

In this chapter, we explored the OpenStack projects at a high level. You learned a little about each of the core projects and some of the optional projects that are deployed. We looked at the main supporting technologies that OpenStack leverages to provide things like, data persistence, and messaging. Finally, we introduced the troubleshooting methodology that we will use throughout this book and a few of the troubleshooting tools that we will take advantage of while working with OpenStack. In the next chapter, we will dive into troubleshooting OpenStack Keystone, the identity service.

2
Troubleshooting OpenStack Identity

Keystone plays a crucial role in the OpenStack deployment. This project is responsible for providing services that support an identity, token management, a service catalog, and policy functionality. While Keystone does not depend on any other OpenStack services, most other OpenStack services depend on Keystone. This core dependency on Keystone means that problems with your Keystone services can cascade, causing problems for many of the other OpenStack services. Tracking down a problem in OpenStack can be complicated due to the different projects that operate together to provide a functionality. When troubleshooting OpenStack, it's smart to make sure that Keystone is operating as intended. In this chapter, we will explore the following topics:

- Identifying different versions of the Keystone API and how to avoid configuration problems
- Troubleshooting the command-line interface clients
- Checking the Identity API
- Fixing issues with the Keystone database
- Confirming the accuracy of the service catalog
- Configuring Keystone to run it as a WSGI application under Apache

Know your version

As of the Liberty release of OpenStack, the identity service finds itself in transition. The service supports two API versions: v2 and v3. The v2 version of the API is deprecated, but may still be found in many OpenStack deployments. Recent releases of OpenStack are configured to serve both the v2 and v3 versions of the Identity API. This can be confirmed by examining the `keystone-paste.ini` configuration file.

```
[composite:main]
use = egg:Paste#urlmap
/v2.0 = public_api
/v3 = api_v3
/ = public_version_api

[composite:admin]
use = egg:Paste#urlmap
/v2.0 = admin_api
/v3 = api_v3
/ = admin_version_api
```

In this file, you will find configurations for two composite apps: main and admin. As demonstrated in the preceding example, each app has a setting for `/v2.0` and `/v3`. With this configuration, this deployment will serve a request to the v2 or v3 Identity API. Here, the command-line clients transition from individual clients per project to a unified OpenStack client that works across projects. The keystone command-line client supports v2 of the Identity API. The newer and preferred OpenStack client supports v2 and v3 of the Identity API.

The two composite apps in the preceding configuration are used to serve two different Keystone APIs: the public API and the admin API. Historically, the admin API was used to serve admin-level requests, such as adding a tenant or adding a user. The functionality of the admin API is small and focused. The public API is responsible for serving all other requests.

With v3 of the Identity API, the separation between the admin functionality and public functionality is handled within a single API. You will notice in the preceding configuration that the `/v3` value is `api_v3` for both the main composite app and the admin composite app.

When Keystone is operating properly, it provides two APIs: the Service API and the Administration API. The Service API runs on port 5000 and the Admin API runs on port 35357. In the OpenStack Juno release and earlier, the common way of running these APIs was via an Eventlet-based process. In the Kilo release and those thereafter, the recommended method to run the Keystone APIs is via a WSGI server. We'll take a look at how to troubleshoot each of these methods in the following sections.

Running Keystone under Eventlet

If you are running Keystone using the Eventlet-based process, you will use the keystone-all command to start the Keystone services. This command will start both the Service API and the Administration API in a single process.

Checking the Keystone service

You can confirm that Keystone was started successfully by running ps -aux | grep keystone, which should show you several keystone-all processes. The output should look similar to the following output:

```
[root@ost-controller:~# ps -aux | grep keystone
root      8106  0.0  0.0  11980    916 pts/6     S+   16:54   0:00 grep keystone
keystone 24969  0.4  1.5 131272 57920 ?          Ss   Feb06  20:39 /usr/bin/python
 /usr/local/bin/keystone-all --config-file=/etc/keystone/keystone.conf --log-fil
e=/var/log/keystone/keystone.log
keystone 24993  0.0  1.7 242712 66496 ?          S    Feb06   0:07 /usr/bin/python
 /usr/local/bin/keystone-all --config-file=/etc/keystone/keystone.conf --log-fil
e=/var/log/keystone/keystone.log
keystone 24994  0.0  1.7 242312 65888 ?          S    Feb06   0:08 /usr/bin/python
 /usr/local/bin/keystone-all --config-file=/etc/keystone/keystone.conf --log-fil
e=/var/log/keystone/keystone.log
keystone 24995  0.0  1.6 241192 64836 ?          S    Feb06   0:00 /usr/bin/python
 /usr/local/bin/keystone-all --config-file=/etc/keystone/keystone.conf --log-fil
e=/var/log/keystone/keystone.log
keystone 24996  0.0  1.7 242220 65780 ?          S    Feb06   0:03 /usr/bin/python
 /usr/local/bin/keystone-all --config-file=/etc/keystone/keystone.conf --log-fil
e=/var/log/keystone/keystone.log
```

You can also check this by running `pgrep -l keystone`. The output from this command should look similar to this output:

```
root@ost-controller:~# pgrep -l keystone
24969 keystone-all
24993 keystone-all
24994 keystone-all
24995 keystone-all
24996 keystone-all
```

Checking the Keystone client

You can use the `openstack` client or the `keystone` command-line client to double check whether Keystone is running properly. Before you use the client, make sure that you have sourced the credentials in your `openrc` file or be prepared to pass the required `auth` attributes in with the command. If you forget to take one of these steps, you may see an error like the following one:

```
root@ost-controller:~# openstack user list
Missing parameter(s):
Set a username with --os-username, OS_USERNAME, or auth.username
Set an authentication URL, with --os-auth-url, OS_AUTH_URL or auth.auth_url
Set a scope, such as a project or domain, set a project scope with --os-project-
name, OS_PROJECT_NAME or auth.project_name, set a domain scope with --os-domain-
name, OS_DOMAIN_NAME or auth.domain_name
```

In the examples that follow, we have sourced the `openrc` file where environment variables have been set for the `auth` attributes. For more information on how to create and source openrc files, refer to the OpenStack documentation at `http://docs.openstack.org/cli-reference/common/cli_set_environment_variables_using_openstack_rc.html` or check out *OpenStack Cloud Computing Cookbook* by Jackson, Bunch, and Sigler.

You can test Keystone by executing the following command:

```
keystone user-list
```

If Keystone is running properly, you will see a list of users that you have loaded into Keystone:

```
+----------------------------------+--------+---------+-------+
|                id                |  name  | enabled | email |
+----------------------------------+--------+---------+-------+
| de698f18d2f44b4bba70dc87c71d3a59 | admin  |  True   |       |
| afd350c5c2c74ffaaf095e8524b14a3a |  ec2   |  True   |       |
| 30214ad3b53c425ba1230814e66a848a | glance |  True   |       |
| 44d5e98f506042cd9c1400244560cd3b |  nova  |  True   |       |
| e61c14e7ab12490495ef80358b604c68 | swift  |  True   |       |
+----------------------------------+--------+---------+-------+
```

Checking the OpenStack Client

You can also use the new OpenStack Client to check Keystone. Run the following OpenStack Client command:

```
openstack user list
```

The value returned should be similar to this one:

 The OpenStack Client is the preferred command-line client when working with OpenStack. This unified client allows users to execute functions across all the OpenStack projects. Nowadays, the historical project-specific command-line clients, such as the keystone client, are being deprecated in favor of the unified OpenStack client.

The client debug mode

The legacy Keystone client and the OpenStack client each have a debug option. You can run a command in the debug mode by passing in the --debug argument. Take this code as an example:

```
keystone --debug tenant-list
```
```
openstack --debug project list
```

Running commands with the --debug argument will cause debug lines to be printed to the console. This debug information may include details of the API request sent by the command-line tool and the response body details sent back from the API. This information often contains useful clues that can aid you in troubleshooting.

Checking the API

To confirm that the APIs have started up on the expected ports, you can run the following curl command to test the API:

```
1   curl -i \
2     -H "Content-Type: application/json" \
3     -d '
4   {
5       "auth": {
6           "identity": {
7               "methods": [
8                   "password"
9               ],
10              "password": {
11                  "user": {
12                      "name": "admin",
13                      "domain": {
14                          "id": "default"
15                      },
16                      "password": "secrete"
17                  }
18              }
19          }
20      }
21  }' \
22      http://localhost:5000/v3/auth/tokens; echo
```

Let's take a closer look at the preceding `curl` command:

- **Line 1**: Here, we call the `curl` command with the -i option, which is the `include` option. It indicates that we want the HTTP-header included in the output.

- **Line 2**: In this line, we set the content type header to be JSON, as the OpenStack API's speak JSON.

- **Line 3**: Here, we use the `-d` option to indicate the data that we are going to POST to the server. Following this line is JSON that we are going to send in the body of our request.

- **Line 8**: Here, we are indicating that we will authenticate with a password.

- **Line 10-16**: In these lines, we provide the password object that includes a user, username, domain, and password.

This API call should return a response similar to the following one:

```
1   {
2       "token": {
3           "methods": [
4               "password"
5           ],
6           "expires_at": "2015-09-07T19:18:50.285110Z",
7           "extras": {},
8           "user": {
9               "domain": {
10                  "id": "default",
11                  "name": "Default"
12              },
13              "id": "1a20622bc0f644d1b79e0d4480143b40",
14              "name": "admin"
15          },
16          "audit_ids": [
17              "8xVWxzEsQFeMoZ9JvuaUCQ"
18          ],
19          "issued_at": "2015-09-07T18:18:50.285217Z"
20      }
21  }
```

- **Line 6**: Here, we have the expiration date/time for the auth token.
- **Line 13**: This line displays the actual auth token that we would use with future requests.

Keystone process not starting

If Keystone doesn't start, there are a couple of areas you want to check. First, check for the keystone processes using pgrep -l keystone or ps -aux | grep keystone, as described in the preceding section. Typically, you will see multiple keystone-all processes running. If you only see one, you may want to double check things. Take a look at the Keystone log file. The log files are located at /var/log/keystone/keystone.log. In the log file, look out for a line similar to this one:

`Parent process has died unexpectedly, exiting`

In addition, when you try to run a command from the Keystone client or the OpenStack client, you may see an error similar to this one:

`Unable to establish connection`

If you try to do a cURL call when Keystone is in this state, you may see an error like the following in response:

`Error code explanation: 501 = Server does not support this operation.`

One of the reasons for the preceding errors is that there is something else running on one of Keystone's ports. Keystone will attempt to start up on ports 5000 and 35357.

You can check which process is running on those ports by running this command:

```
lsof -i :35357 -S
```

The following output shows Keystone listening on port 35357:

```
COMMAND     PID      USER    FD   TYPE DEVICE SIZE/OFF NODE NAME
keystone- 24969 keystone    7u   IPv4  59964      0t0  TCP *:35357 (LISTEN)
keystone- 24993 keystone    7u   IPv4  59964      0t0  TCP *:35357 (LISTEN)
keystone- 24994 keystone    7u   IPv4  59964      0t0  TCP *:35357 (LISTEN)
keystone- 24995 keystone    7u   IPv4  59964      0t0  TCP *:35357 (LISTEN)
keystone- 24996 keystone    7u   IPv4  59964      0t0  TCP *:35357 (LISTEN)
```

```
lsof -i :5000 -S
```

The following output from the preceding command shows Keystone listening on port 5000:

```
COMMAND     PID      USER    FD   TYPE DEVICE SIZE/OFF NODE NAME
keystone- 24969 keystone    8u   IPv4  59965      0t0  TCP *:5000 (LISTEN)
keystone- 24995 keystone    8u   IPv4  59965      0t0  TCP *:5000 (LISTEN)
keystone- 24996 keystone    8u   IPv4  59965      0t0  TCP *:5000 (LISTEN)
```

Finally, you can attempt to start Keystone manually and check whether any errors are printed to the console during startup. To start Keystone manually, you would run a command similar to the following one, taking a note to modify the configuration values in order to match your deployment:

```
sudo -u keystone /usr/local/bin/keystone-all --config-file=/etc/keystone/
keystone.conf  --log-file=/var/log/keystone/keystone.log
```

Database stopped

Consider a situation where Keystone appears to have started but hangs when you run a command such as keystone tenant-list and eventually returns with an error similar to this:

```
Authorization Failed: An unexpected error prevented the server from
fulfilling your request. (HTTP 500)
```

Or, consider a situation where your API calls return with an error similar to this:

```
HTTP/1.1 500 Internal Server Error
Vary: X-Auth-Token
Content-Type: application/json
Content-Length: 143
X-Openstack-Request-Id: req-98cb32c0-c942-41c7-9a3d-90e6aed95eb3
Date: Tue, 08 Sep 2015 02:53:00 GMT
{"error": {"message": "An unexpected error prevented the server from
fulfilling your request.", "code": 500, "title": "Internal Server
Error"}}
```

In such cases, we need to check the Keystone log file that is typically located at `/var/log/keystone/keystone.log`. Be on the lookout for `DBConnectionError`.

If your logs contain this error, make sure that your database is up and running and accessible at the address and port recorded in the `keystone.conf` configuration file. You can find the database string in the section of the `config` file labeled `[database]`. The configuration option is titled `connection`. Double check the database configuration string to make sure it is correct; then, make sure that the database is running and accessible. An example of the database section in `keystone.conf` looks like this:

```
[database]
connection = mysql://keystone:keystone@mydbserver.com/keystone
```

You can try to connect to the database directly in order to confirm that it is running and configured as expected. You can connect to `mysql` using a command like the following one:

```
mysql -u keystone -p -h mydbserver.com keystone
```

You will be prompted for a password, at which time you should enter the same password that appears between : and @ in your connection string. Once you are connected to the Keystone database in MySQL, you can run the show tables command to confirm that the Keystone tables have been created. If this command comes back empty, this means that you need to initialize your database. To initialize the Keystone database, we leverage a command-line tool called keystone-manage. The database is initialized when you run the following command:

```
keystone-manage db_sync
```

The service catalog endpoint

One potential source of problems with Keystone is the misconfiguration of Keystone endpoints. One of the functions that Keystone provides for OpenStack is the Service Catalog functionality. The service catalog tracks and displays all the endpoints for each of the OpenStack services including Keystone itself. You can view the endpoint entry for Keystone by running this:

```
openstack endpoint show keystone
```

This command will return something similar to the following output:

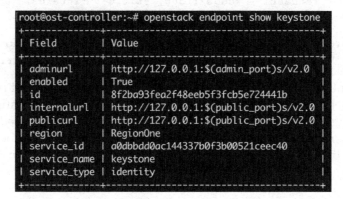

Check the ports for `adminurl`, making sure that it is using the admin port, which is 35357 or `$(admin_port)/s`. Check the `internalurl` and `publicurl` ports and make sure they are set to 5000 or `$(public_port)/s`. If the ports are configured incorrectly on the endpoints, this could result in we not being able to execute Keystone functions.

Running under WSGI

With the Kilo release of OpenStack, the recommended method to run the Keystone API is via WSGI, for example, an Apache web server running the `mod_wsgi` module. If you run into trouble while running Keystone via WSGI, there are a few things you want to check, which are listed as follows:

1. Make sure that the `mod_wsgi` Apache module is installed

2. Check `wsgi-keystone.conf`

3. Check the `keystone-wsgi-admin` and `keystone-wsgi-public` files

4. Confirm that Keystone is not running under Eventlet

mod_wsgi

First, make sure that you source your credentials in your `openrc` file; then, try to run one of the keystone commands:

```
openstack user list
keystone user-list
```

If you get an Invalid command error like the one listed in the following code, make sure you install `mod_wsgi`:

```
Invalid command 'WSGIDaemonProcess', perhaps misspelled or defined by a
module not included in the server configuration
```

You can install `mod_wsgi` as follows:

```
apt-get install libapache2-mod-wsgi
```

wsgi-keystone.conf

Second, make sure you have the `wsgi-keystone.conf` file copied to the `/etc/apache2/sites-available` directory. An example of this file is located at `http://tinyurl.com/jnobwbt`.

Also, make sure that you have symlinked the `/etc/apache2/sites-available/wsgi-keystone.conf` file to `/etc/apache2/sites-enabled/wsgi-keystone.conf`. You can accomplish this by running this code snippet:

```
ln -s /etc/apache2/sites-available/wsgi-keystone.conf /etc/apache2/sites-
enabled
```

 The preceding command returns no output when it is completed successfully. You can confirm that it was successful by running `ls -l`, where you will see the symlink.

Stopping the Eventlet process

When you attempt to start Apache with the new `wsgi-keystone.conf` file and you receive this error, make sure you don't have the Eventlet version of Keystone running:

```
(98)Address already in use: AH00072: make_sock: could not bind to address
[::]:5000
```

```
(98)Address already in use: AH00072: make_sock: could not bind to address
0.0.0.0:5000
```

```
no listening sockets available, shutting down
```

You can stop the Eventlet process by running the following command:

```
stop keystone
```

After stopping the Keystone Eventlet process, restart Apache and watch /var/log/apache2/keystone.log to confirm that the service has started successfully.

Checking WSGI files

If you attempt to run the Openstack user list and you receive an error like the following one, check the keystone.log file in Apache:

```
Authorization Failed: Not Found (HTTP 404)
```

On Ubuntu, this file is located at /var/log/apache2/keystone.log.

```
2016-02-16 11:48:49.501084 Target WSGI script not found or unable to stat:
 /usr/local/bin/keystone-wsgi-admin
2016-02-16 11:48:49.503085 Target WSGI script not found or unable to stat:
 /usr/local/bin/keystone-wsgi-admin
```

If you see the preceding error, you need to do the following:

- Check the paths and location of the WSGI files in the WSGIScriptAlias attribute of /etc/apache2/sites-available/wsgi-keystone.conf
- Make sure that the keystone-wsgi-admin and keystone-wsgi-public files exist in the /usr/local/bin/ directory

Checking the Keystone service

Much like we did when running Keystone with Eventlet, we can also check the Keystone service when running it under WSGI by executing the following command:

```
ps -aux | grep keystone
```

When running Keystone in Apache, the results of this command will look similar to the following output:

```
root@ost-controller:~# ps -aux | grep keystone
root      6229  0.0  0.0  11980    916 pts/2   R+   18:56   0:00 grep keys
tone
keystone 12213  0.0  0.1 178508   5068 ?       Sl   13:41   0:00 (wsgi:key
stone-pu -k start
keystone 12214  0.0  0.1 178516   5080 ?       Sl   13:41   0:00 (wsgi:key
stone-pu -k start
keystone 12215  0.0  0.1 178508   5080 ?       Sl   13:41   0:00 (wsgi:key
stone-pu -k start
keystone 12216  0.0  0.1 178508   5080 ?       Sl   13:41   0:00 (wsgi:key
stone-pu -k start
keystone 12217  0.0  0.1 178508   5080 ?       Sl   13:41   0:00 (wsgi:key
stone-pu -k start
keystone 12218  0.0  1.6 430788  64752 ?       Sl   13:41   0:02 (wsgi:key
stone-ad -k start
keystone 12219  0.0  1.6 430276  64136 ?       Sl   13:41   0:02 (wsgi:key
stone-ad -k start
keystone 12220  0.0  1.6 430020  63720 ?       Sl   13:41   0:02 (wsgi:key
stone-ad -k start
keystone 12221  0.0  1.6 430276  64244 ?       Sl   13:41   0:02 (wsgi:key
stone-ad -k start
keystone 12222  0.0  1.6 430532  64584 ?       Sl   13:41   0:02 (wsgi:key
stone-ad -k start
```

If you happen to run this command and it doesn't return wsgi processes, you will want to make sure that Apache is running and that Keystone has been correctly configured to run under WSGI.

Summary

In this chapter, we looked at how to resolve common issues with the Identity service. We learned how to tell which version of the Keystone API we are using and also looked at how to use the command-line interface clients to troubleshoot. We made calls to the Identity API in order to confirm that Keystone was running as expected and learned to troubleshoot issues with the Keystone database. We also checked the service catalog to make sure endpoints were properly configured and successfully ran Keystone as a WSGI application under Apache.

Keystone plays a central role in the successful operation of an OpenStack cluster. Each of the other OpenStack services depend on Keystone and the functionality it provides. As a result, successful troubleshooters will need to make sure that Keystone is running correctly. In the next chapter, we will look at how to troubleshoot the OpenStack Image service, code named Glance.

3
Troubleshooting the OpenStack Image Service

Glance is the code name for the OpenStack image service. This service is responsible for the functionality that allows users to discover virtual machine images, register new images, and retrieve existing images. Glance provides a RESTful API, which also powers the command-line interface and the image functionality in the Horizon Dashboard.

In this chapter, we will systematically walk you through the troubleshooting layers, which are as follows:

- Glance services
- The Glance database
- The Glance authentication
- The Glance API
- The Glance command-line client
- Glance logging and configuration
- Common errors

Glance is made up of several components. There is an API service and a registry service included in Glance. Each of these services need to be running for Glance to work properly. Glance also requires a database such as MySQL or Postgres. Finally, Glance supports several storage backends, where images are physically stored. The backend you use is configurable in `glance-api.conf`.

Glance services

When troubleshooting Glance, one of the first things to check is whether or not the service is running. A quick way to confirm this is by running some simple Glance commands from the command line:

```
glance image-list
```

When Glance operates properly, this command should return a list of images in your Glance repository, similar to the following output:

This command may also return an empty list if your Glance repository is empty. You may receive an error when you run this command that is similar to the following error:

```
You must provide a username via either --os-username or env[OS_USERNAME]
```

This error typically occurs when you haven't passed all the necessary attributes to the `glance image-list` command. The common way to solve this problem is by creating an `openrc` file that contains the attributes that are required by the command-line client. A sample `openrc` file would look like this:

```
1  export OS_USERNAME=admin
2  export OS_PASSWORD=mysupersecretpassword
3  export OS_TENANT_NAME=demo
4  export OS_AUTH_URL=http://my.ip.address:35357/v2.0
5  export OS_REGION_NAME=RegionOne
```

Once you adjust the preceding lines to include your specific details, you would save that content to a file named `openrc`. To leverage these settings, simply source the `openrc` file:

```
source openrc
```

Once the `openrc` file has been sourced, you should be able to run commands such as `glance image-list` without the need to provide the required attributes on the command line. When you run the Glance `image-list` command and you see an error similar to the following one, you should confirm that the Glance service is running:

```
Error finding address for http://127.0.0.1:9292/versions: HTTPConnectionPo
ol(host='127.0.0.1', port=9292): Max retries exceeded with url: /versions
(Caused by NewConnectionError('<requests.packages.urllib3.connection.HTTPC
onnection object at 0x7f52d3cece10>: Failed to establish a new connection:
[Errno 111] Connection refused',))
```

There are a few ways in which you can verify that Glance is running. You can check for the Glance processes by running this command:

```
ps -aux | grep glance-
```

When Glance is running successfully, you will see a process for the `glance-api` and `glance-registry`. The output will look similar to the following output:

```
root@ost-controller:~# ps -aux | grep glance-
root      15749  6.2  2.0 173692 80780 ?        Ss   15:23   0:01 /usr/bin/
python /usr/local/bin/glance-api
root      15750  4.0  1.8 148240 72004 ?        Ss   15:23   0:00 /usr/bin/
python /usr/local/bin/glance-registry
root      15769  0.0  1.7 148240 68952 ?        S    15:23   0:00 /usr/bin/
python /usr/local/bin/glance-registry
root      15771  0.0  1.7 148240 68952 ?        S    15:23   0:00 /usr/bin/
python /usr/local/bin/glance-registry
root      15794  0.0  2.0 173692 77548 ?        S    15:23   0:00 /usr/bin/
python /usr/local/bin/glance-api
root      15795  0.0  2.0 173692 77548 ?        S    15:23   0:00 /usr/bin/
python /usr/local/bin/glance-api
root      15996  0.0  0.0  11980   920 pts/0    S+   15:24   0:00 grep glan
ce-
```

If you find that the `glance-api` and `glance-registry` processes are not running, you can use the glance-control tool to start them. To start all the Glance services, simply run this command:

```
glance-control all start
```

This command will start the Glance API and the Glance Registry.

Confirming the Glance database

Once you have confirmed that the Glance service has started properly, you should verify that the database is configured and operating properly. Begin by confirming that your database engine is running. You can check whether `mysql` is running by executing the following command:

```
service mysql status
```

```
mysql start/running, process 15628
```

If this command does not return a message indicating that the process is running, you will need to troubleshoot your database server to get it working properly. How to troubleshoot your database engine is outside the scope of this book, but there are many great resources out there that can help.

Next, you should confirm that you can connect to the database server. For example, to confirm that you can connect to MySQL, use a command similar to the following one:

```
mysql -u db_user -p -h my.db.server glance
```

Be sure to replace db_user with a valid username for your database and replace my_db_server with the hostname or IP address of your database. The last argument to this command is the database name, which in this case is glance. If you are successfully connected to MySQL, you will see an output similar to what is displayed here:

```
Welcome to the MySQL monitor.  Commands end with ; or \g.
Your MySQL connection id is 95
Server version: 5.5.47-0ubuntu0.14.04.1 (Ubuntu)

Copyright (c) 2000, 2015, Oracle and/or its affiliates. All rights reserve
d.

Oracle is a registered trademark of Oracle Corporation and/or its
affiliates. Other names may be trademarks of their respective
owners.

Type 'help;' or '\h' for help. Type '\c' to clear the current input statem
ent.

mysql>
```

If you are unsuccessful when trying to connect to the database manually, be sure to verify the username and password of the database user you are utilizing. Once the credentials are confirmed, you should also check whether the user has appropriate privileges to access this database. With MySQL, you can leverage the show grants statement:

```
mysql> show grants for 'glance'@'localhost';
+-------------------------------------------------------------------
-----------------------------+
| Grants for glance@localhost
                                              |
+-------------------------------------------------------------------
-----------------------------+
| GRANT USAGE ON *.* TO 'glance'@'localhost' IDENTIFIED BY PASSWORD '*CC67
CAF178CB9A07D756302E0BBFA3B0165DFD49' |
| GRANT ALL PRIVILEGES ON `glance`.* TO 'glance'@'localhost'
                                              |
+-------------------------------------------------------------------
-----------------------------+
2 rows in set (0.00 sec)
```

The database user for the glance database in our case is named glance. We have
ensured that our glance user has all the privileges on the database, which is also
named glance.

In addition to having your database engine up and running, we need to confirm that
the glance database exists. In MySQL, when you run the show databases command,
glance should be in the list:

```
mysql> show databases;
+--------------------+
| Database           |
+--------------------+
| information_schema |
| glance             |
| heat               |
| keystone           |
| mysql              |
| neutron            |
| nova               |
| performance_schema |
+--------------------+
8 rows in set (0.00 sec)
```

If the glance database does not appear in the database list, then you simply need to create an empty database named `glance`. After confirming that the glance database exists, you also need to ensure that it is properly initialized. An initialized Glance database will have several tables created. You can confirm this in MySQL by running the show tables command in the database named `glance`:

```
mysql> show tables;
+------------------------------------------+
| Tables_in_glance                         |
+------------------------------------------+
| artifact_blob_locations                  |
| artifact_blobs                           |
| artifact_dependencies                    |
| artifact_properties                      |
| artifact_tags                            |
| artifacts                                |
| image_locations                          |
| image_members                            |
| image_properties                         |
| image_tags                               |
| images                                   |
| metadef_namespace_resource_types         |
| metadef_namespaces                       |
| metadef_objects                          |
| metadef_properties                       |
| metadef_resource_types                   |
| metadef_tags                             |
| migrate_version                          |
| task_info                                |
| tasks                                    |
+------------------------------------------+
20 rows in set (0.00 sec)
```

When you run this command, if it returns an empty list, you need to initialize your glance database. This can be achieved by running the following command:

```
glance-manage db_sync
```

This command will output several logging messages to the terminal, as it executes the database initialization. Upon completion, you should be able to run the show tables command again and see a list of tables similar to the preceding list.

Finally, you should confirm that the database connection string is configured properly in the `glance-api.conf` file located in the `127.0.0.1/glance` directory. You can quickly view the current configuration for this connection string by running the following command:

```
less /etc/glance/glance-api.conf | grep ^connection
```

The result of this command will be similar to the following output:

```
connection = mysql://glance_db_user:glance_db_pass@
```

After this, confirm the database username and password used in the connection string. If you haven't already, follow the steps at the beginning of this section to connect to your database, using the same username and password indicated in your `glance-api` configuration file.

Confirming the Glance authentication

Glance requires Keystone for its authentication. For Glance to work properly, Keystone needs to be configured and run properly. For details on troubleshooting Keystone, refer to the previous chapter in this book. To confirm that Glance and Keystone are successfully working together, follow these steps.

Keystone up

Make sure Keystone is running. You can confirm this by running the following command:

```
ps -aux | grep keystone
```

This command should return an output similar to the following:

```
root@ost-controller:~# ps -aux | grep keystone
root       5344  0.0  0.0  11980    920 pts/0    S+   15:51   0:00 grep keys
tone
keystone  16429  0.0  0.1 178516   5068 ?        Sl   12:41   0:00 (wsgi:key
stone-pu -k start
keystone  16430  0.0  0.1 178508   5080 ?        Sl   12:41   0:00 (wsgi:key
stone-pu -k start
keystone  16431  0.0  0.1 178508   5080 ?        Sl   12:41   0:00 (wsgi:key
stone-pu -k start
keystone  16432  0.0  0.1 178508   5080 ?        Sl   12:41   0:00 (wsgi:key
stone-pu -k start
keystone  16433  0.0  0.1 178508   5080 ?        Sl   12:41   0:00 (wsgi:key
stone-pu -k start
keystone  16437  0.0  1.7 431044  67124 ?        Sl   12:41   0:02 (wsgi:key
stone-ad -k start
keystone  16438  0.0  1.7 431044  67432 ?        Sl   12:41   0:02 (wsgi:key
stone-ad -k start
keystone  16439  0.0  1.7 431300  67608 ?        Sl   12:41   0:02 (wsgi:key
stone-ad -k start
keystone  16440  0.0  1.7 431300  67664 ?        Sl   12:41   0:02 (wsgi:key
stone-ad -k start
keystone  16444  0.0  1.7 430788  66816 ?        Sl   12:41   0:02 (wsgi:key
stone-ad -k start
```

If you do not see any Keystone processes running, refer to the previous chapter in this book for Keystone troubleshooting tips.

Service User Set Up

The service user setup

By convention, most OpenStack deployments will have users created for each service. In this case, it would be a Glance service user named `glance`. Confirm that this user exists by running the following command:

```
openstack user list
```

Running this command will return a list of users in Keystone. An example of the output is given in the following code:

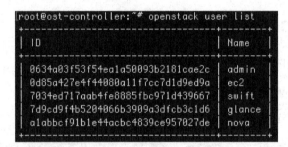

Make sure that there is a user named `glance`. Secondly, this user should belong to a `project/tenant` named `service` by convention. You can confirm that the service project exists by running the following command:

```
openstack project list
```

This command will list the projects (tenants) configured in our Keystone installation:

In the output of this command, you should see a project named `service`, as demonstrated in the preceding code. The next step is to confirm that the glance user is assigned to this project. The next command will accomplish this:

```
openstack user show glance
```

The preceding `user show` command will display details for the `glance` user:

In the preceding `project_id` field, we are looking for a project ID that matches the ID of our `service` project displayed in the OpenStack project list command we ran earlier. In our example, the project ID we are looking for is `7d9cdf4b5204066b3909a3dfcb3c1d6`. The output tells us that our glance user is indeed a part of the `service` project.

Next, we need to confirm that the `glance` user has the correct roles in Keystone. The following command can help us with this:

```
openstack user role list --project service glance
```

This command will list the roles for the `glance` user in the context of the `service` project:

```
root@ost-controller:~# openstack user role list --project service glance
+-----------------------------------+----------+---------+--------+
| ID                                | Name     | Project | User   |
+-----------------------------------+----------+---------+--------+
| 9fe2ff9ee4384b1894a90878d3e92bab  | _member_ | service | glance |
| c81d41b2cd0940a09b4aeaa331057f25  | admin    | service | glance |
+-----------------------------------+----------+---------+--------+
```

When examining the output of this command, we want to confirm that the glance user has the admin role in the service project.

Finally, let's confirm the password for the glance user. A quick way to confirm the password is using the OpenStack command-line client, authenticating as the glance user. To achieve this, we will run a command similar to the following one:

```
openstack --os-username glance --os-password glance --os-project-name
service project list
```

The preceding command is really just the OpenStack project list command with a few arguments passed in on the command line. The arguments passed in will override the values we have in our `openrc` file. This allows us to test different users, which are stated as follows:

- `--os-username`: This indicates the username of the user we want to use. For this test, the username is `glance`.

- `--os-password`: This is the value we are targeting with this test. We want to make sure that the password is set and working as expected. For my test, I'm expecting the password to also be `glance`.

- `--os-project-name`: Finally, we need to pass in the project name so that Keystone knows which project to authenticate. Our user may have different roles under different projects. In our example, we are testing the `glance` user under the `service` project.

If the password for the `glance` user is indeed `glance`, as I expect, this command will return a list of projects in Keystone:

```
root@ost-controller:~# openstack --os-username glance --os-password glance
 --os-project-name service project list
+----------------------------------+---------+
| ID                               | Name    |
+----------------------------------+---------+
| e0361c137eab40a8834ab772ce5fdf06 | demo    |
| 1f9e6ced0ea74c7e8c5839451d16a096 | service |
+----------------------------------+---------+
```

This error tells me that the password is probably not `glance`, as I anticipated:

```
The request you have made requires authentication. (HTTP 401)
(Request-ID: req-707fd197-ae15-4698-ac04-1de4c92acfe9)
```

At this point, I can try a few more password possibilities or I can reset the password. To reset the glance user's password, you can use a command like the following one:

```
openstack user set --password-prompt glance
```

When you run the preceding command, you will be prompted to enter a new password for the glance user and then asked to type that password a second time to confirm. After you reset the password, you can test it using the same technique we described earlier.

The final step is to confirm that our credentials are set properly in the glance configuration files. In both the /etc/glance/glance-api.conf and the /etc/glance/glance-registry.conf file, there should be a keystone_authtoken stanza. Under that stanza, if auth_plugin = password, make sure that the values of the username and password field match the values you have set in Keystone:

```
1   [keystone_authtoken]
2   ...
3   auth_plugin = password
4   username = glance
5   password = glance
6   ...
```

In the preceding example, our username is set to glance and our password is set to glance. Replace these values with the username and password you have configured for your installation.

Service endpoints correct

At this stage, we should confirm that the service catalog contains the correct endpoints for the Glance service:

```
openstack endpoint show glance
```

When you run the endpoint show command as demonstrated in the preceding line of code, you will see details for the glance endpoint in the service catalog. An example of a typical output is included in the following code snippet:

```
root@ost-controller:~# openstack endpoint show glance
+--------------+----------------------------------+
| Field        | Value                            |
+--------------+----------------------------------+
| adminurl     | http://127.0.0.1:9292            |
| enabled      | True                             |
| id           | e5e67d9a525a46209ae6792cfb58f41c |
| internalurl  | http://127.0.0.1:9292            |
| publicurl    | http://127.0.0.1:9292            |
| region       | RegionOne                        |
| service_id   | 0c7012c678014aa58bb58cc302391cb8 |
| service_name | glance                           |
| service_type | image                            |
+--------------+----------------------------------+
```

Confirm that the values of the `adminurl`, `internalurl`, and `publicurl` are correct. If any of these values are incorrect, you have the following three options to correct the issue:

- You can use the `openstack endpoint delete` command to remove the current endpoints, followed by the `openstack endpoint create` command.

- If you are using the default SQL driver for your service catalog, you can make the edits to the endpoints directly in the SQL database. Use caution when executing this option.

- If you are using the templated driver for your service catalog, you simply need to update your endpoint template file.

Confirming the Glance API setup

You can confirm that Glance is running as expected by testing the Glance API. This will also allow you to confirm that Glance and Keystone are correctly configured to work together. To begin, you can request an Auth Token using the Keystone API and your `glance` service user. If you have any trouble with getting Keystone to run successfully, refer to *Chapter 2, Troubleshooting OpenStack Identity*. The following CURL request will generate an auth token for the `glance` service user:

```
curl -i \
  -H "Content-Type: application/json" \
  -d '
    {"auth": {
        "identity": {
            "methods": [
                "password"
            ],
            "password": {
                "user": {
                    "name": "glance",
                    "domain": {
                        "id": "default"
                    },
                    "password": "glance"
                }
            }
        },
        "scope": {
            "project": {
                "name": "service",
                "domain": {
                    "id": "default"
                }
            }
        }
    }' \
  http://127.0.0.1:5000/v3/auth/tokens ; echo
```

Make sure to modify the preceding cURL call with your `glance` user's password and the correct IP address or URL for your keystone installation. In the preceding example, I used `glance` as the password for the glance service user and localhost in the URL for my Keystone endpoint.

This `Curl` command will return a scoped token from Keystone. The headers returned in response will be similar to the following output:

```
HTTP/1.1 201 Created
Date: Wed, 17 Feb 2016 20:27:58 GMT
Server: Apache/2.4.7 (Ubuntu)
X-Subject-Token: 24de2acda0a54704992995567fd54cae
Vary: X-Auth-Token
x-openstack-request-id: req-39c32eaa-4e31-4a92-a0d8-e2bf45c78179
Content-Length: 4262
Content-Type: application/json
```

The `Auth Token` is contained in the header name `X-Subject-Token`. We will use this Auth Token when we query the Glance API to confirm that it is working properly. To test the Glance API, we send a request to list the images in Glance:

```
1  curl -s \
2      -H "Accept: application/json" \
3      -H "Content-Type: application/json" \
4      -H 'X-Auth-Token: 24de2acda0a54704992995567fd54cae' \
5          http://127.0.0.1:9292/v2/images
```

This API request will return a response that is similar to the following one:

```
1  {
2      "first": "/v2/images",
3      "images": [
4          {
5              "checksum": "ee1eca47dc88f4879d8a229cc70a07c6",
6              "container_format": "bare",
7              "created_at": "2016-02-17T04:22:36Z",
8              "disk_format": "qcow2",
9              "file": "/v2/images/784c3873-4900-4767-a2a7-d26e82afefd1/file",
10             "id": "784c3873-4900-4767-a2a7-d26e82afefd1",
11             "min_disk": 0,
12             "min_ram": 0,
13             "name": "cirros-qcow2",
14             "owner": "ee4af31b791f4137b082e6e2d8d20f95",
15             "protected": false,
16             "schema": "/v2/schemas/image",
17             "self": "/v2/images/784c3873-4900-4767-a2a7-d26e82afefd1",
18             "size": 13287936,
19             "status": "active",
20             "tags": [],
21             "updated_at": "2016-02-17T04:22:36Z",
22             "virtual_size": null,
23             "visibility": "public"
24         }
25     ],
26     "schema": "/v2/schemas/images"
27 }
```

Checking the command-line interface client

Now that we have confirmed that the API is working, we will check the command-line interface client and ensure its proper operation. We can begin by listing the images currently registered in Glance. To do this, we will leverage the `openstack image list` command:

```
openstack image list
```

> When using command-line clients, we recommend that you leverage an `openrc` file that contains environment variables representing the required fields of the CLI client. Refer to the *Chapter 2, Troubleshooting OpenStack Identity,* for more information.

On executing this command, you should see a list of images currently registered in Glance, as demonstrated in the following code:

If you do not see an output similar to the preceding one, then there are a few things we need to check. First, if you receive any errors when running this command, carefully go over this section again and confirm that everything is set up as expected. Next, run the command again, but use the `--debug` switch for additional debugging output on the terminal:

```
openstack --debug image list
```

The preceding command should print out several lines of useful information on the terminal.

A few errors that you may come across in this situation include the following:

- **Service Unavailable (HTTP 503)**: This could mean that your password for the glance service user is incorrect. Use the methods discussed in this section to troubleshoot that issue.

- **Unable to establish connection to http://glanceserver:9292/v2/images**: This could be an indication that your Glance API service is not running. Again, you can use the information we covered earlier to help you troubleshoot.

If running the OpenStack image list command does not return an error, but simply returns a blank output, this probably means that you do not have any images in your Glance installation yet.

It's also helpful to have a known working image that you can use for troubleshooting. We can install a Cirros image for this purpose. You can use the following command to download a copy of the Cirros image:

```
wget http://download.cirros-cloud.net/0.3.4/cirros-0.3.4-x86_64-disk.img
```

Once you've downloaded the image, you can load it into Glance using the Glance command-line client:

```
openstack image create --disk-format qcow2 --container-format bare
--public --file cirros-0.3.4-x86_64-disk.img cirros-qcow2
```

Running this command will return an output similar to this:

```
[root@ost-controller:~# openstack image create --disk-format qcow2 --contai
ner-format bare --public --file cirros-0.3.4-x86_64-disk.img cirros-qcow2
+------------------+------------------------------------------------------+
| Field            | Value                                                |
+------------------+------------------------------------------------------+
| checksum         | ee1eca47dc88f4879d8a229cc70a07c6                     |
| container_format | bare                                                 |
| created_at       | 2016-02-17T21:04:14Z                                 |
| disk_format      | qcow2                                                |
| file             | /v2/images/b9a49bfd-bc11-469f-8a3d-                  |
|                  | 44b81e9a5677/file                                    |
| id               | b9a49bfd-bc11-469f-8a3d-44b81e9a5677                 |
| min_disk         | 0                                                    |
| min_ram          | 0                                                    |
| name             | cirros-qcow2                                         |
| owner            | 12cd25cc52c048dcad1c69aa6afe597a                     |
| protected        | False                                                |
| schema           | /v2/schemas/image                                    |
| size             | 13287936                                             |
| status           | active                                               |
| tags             |                                                      |
| updated_at       | 2016-02-17T21:04:14Z                                 |
| virtual_size     | None                                                 |
| visibility       | public                                               |
+------------------+------------------------------------------------------+
```

You can confirm that the image has been successfully loaded by executing the openstack image list command again. Once you have confirmed that the image list command is working, try a few other openstack image commands for extra assurance.

Glance logging and configuration

If, after working your way through each of the preceding sections, you continue to have trouble with Glance, here are a few more elements you should check. The Glance log files will often contain clues that can assist with troubleshooting. You can determine the location of the Glance log files by checking the value of the `log_file` or `log_dir` setting in the Glance configuration file. Typically, the log files for Glance will be located in the `/var/log/glance/` directory. In this directory, you should find several log files including these:

- `api.log`
- `registry.log`

The `api.log` file will likely contain a bulk of clues that you need to troubleshoot Glance. It's also worth reminding you that Glance leverages Keystone for authentication. Therefore, in addition to the Glance logs, you will want to keep an eye on the Keystone logs. Similar to the Glance logs, the Keystone logs are typically located at `/var/log/keystone`. Refer to *Chapter 2*, *Troubleshooting OpenStack Identity*, for more details.

The log level

When troubleshooting OpenStack, it is helpful to increase the logging level so that more information is printed on the logs. This additional information can help provide more insight into how the system is operating and may help you isolate the source of problems. To turn on debug logging for Glance, you need to modify `/etc/glance/glance-api.conf`. In this configuration file, there is a setting named `debug` and is usually located under the `From oslo.log` section. To turn on debugging, simply set `debug = true`.

Where to look

When troubleshooting Glance, it makes sense to start by looking in the Glance logs. However, remember that Glance is interconnected with other OpenStack projects. This means that the root of the problem I am troubleshooting may not be in Glance at all. Therefore, I recommend that you look for log files that have been recently modified. One way to accomplish this is using the `find` command to list log files that have been modified in the last 5 minutes. For example, you can run the following command from the `/var/log` directory to do so:

```
find . -iname "*.log" -mmin -1 -printf '%T+ %p\n' | sort -r
```

An example of what the output will look like is given in the following command:

```
[root@ost-controller:/var/log# find . -iname "*.log" -mmin -1 -printf '%T+
%p\n' | sort -r
2016-02-17+15:55:03.7229414120 ./upstart/neutron-openvswitch.log
2016-02-17+15:55:03.7229414120 ./neutron/openvswitch-agent.log
2016-02-17+15:55:03.7229414120 ./auth.log
2016-02-17+15:54:55.0428722660 ./upstart/neutron-server.log
2016-02-17+15:54:55.0428722660 ./neutron/server.log
2016-02-17+15:54:55.0388722340 ./upstart/neutron-metadata-agent.log
2016-02-17+15:54:55.0388722340 ./neutron/metadata-agent.log
2016-02-17+15:54:53.8268625790 ./upstart/neutron-l3-agent.log
2016-02-17+15:54:53.8228625470 ./neutron/l3-agent.log
2016-02-17+15:54:50.4028353020 ./conntrackd-stats.log
2016-02-17+15:54:49.0668246580 ./upstart/heat-engine.log
2016-02-17+15:54:49.0668246580 ./heat/heat.log
2016-02-17+15:54:47.6988137600 ./upstart/neutron-dhcp-agent.log
2016-02-17+15:54:47.6988137600 ./neutron/dhcp-agent.log
2016-02-17+15:54:12.6305343700 ./upstart/nova-compute.log
2016-02-17+15:54:12.6305343700 ./nova/nova-compute.log
```

Using this command will help you see which log files you may want to investigate for clues.

Searching logs

Again, when troubleshooting Glance, we should start with the Glance log files and then potentially investigate some of the other log files returned from your find command. Once you are ready to start searching through your log files, you can leverage your standard Linux tools to look for useful information. One of the first tools I pick up is the `tail` command. I typically begin by tailing the related log files. For example, when trying to fix a Glance issue, I will tail `glance-api.log`:

```
tail -f /var/log/glance/api.log
```

Another useful tool is grep. I know grep is often seen as a solution and a problem at the same time, but I find it useful when trying to cut through the noise of the OpenStack logs and it also useful to find the useful signals that will assist with troubleshooting. For example, you can grep the log files for the words critical, error, warning, and failure:

```
grep -irE 'critical|error|warning|failure' /var/log/glance/api.log
```

Searching the log files this way can help you quickly isolate and focus on the log lines that provide key information for troubleshooting.

Common errors

In this section, we will explore a few of the more common errors we may come across in the Glance log files. The different errors you may come across are varied, and part of the troubleshooter's job is tracking down the root cause of those errors.

Unable to establish connection

When using the OpenStack client to execute Glance-related commands, you can come across a connection error similar to the following one:

```
Discovering versions from the identity service failed when creating the pa
ssword plugin. Attempting to determine version from URL.
Unable to establish connection to http://localhost:35357/v2.0/tokens
```

This typically indicates a configuration problem wherein Keystone is not accessible at the provided URI. When using the Glance client, this value is typically pulled from the OS_AUTH_URL value in the openrc file. Refer to *Chapter 2, Troubleshooting OpenStack Identity*, for information about the openrc file. You can find yourself in this situation when the value of your os_auth_url is incorrect. Alternately, this could also be the result of Keystone not running on the expected URI and port. To correct this issue, you will need to update your openrc file with the correct os_auth_url or pass the correct value in as an attribute to your OpenStack CLI commands.

Internal server errors (HTTP 500)

Internal server errors in OpenStack can be tricky because there are several factors that may contribute to these problems. In the context of Glance, if you see an error similar to this, be sure to check the database, making sure that it is running and configured correctly:

```
Internal Server Error (HTTP 500) (Request-ID: req-1f2d96b9-480e-4fb8-90be-
71cf02b5f224)
```

Unable to validate token

When you are searching through your logs, if you come across an error like the following one, this is a clue that there is a problem with the configuration between Glance and Keystone:

```
CRITICAL keystonemiddleware.auth_token [-] Unable to validate token
```

If you come across an error like the preceding error, take a look at the `/var/log/glance/api.log` file. Near this error, look out for a log line similar to the following one:

```
DiscoveryFailure: Could not determine a suitable URL for the plugin
```

This error points to the need to confirm your `auth_url` setting in the `glance-api.conf` file. The value for this setting should be the URL for your Keystone installation that is accessed on port `35357`.

Summary

Glance is fairly straightforward and shouldn't be the source of too much trouble in your OpenStack cluster. However, if you do run into trouble, the tactics you have learned in this chapter should help you quickly troubleshoot those issues. By systematically checking the Glance services, database, authentication settings, API, and command-line interface, you should be able to quickly isolate problems and resolve them. In the next chapter, we will be looking into Neutron, the OpenStack Networking Service.

4
Troubleshooting OpenStack Networking

Neutron is an OpenStack networking service. Neutron can be one of the most difficult OpenStack projects to troubleshoot. The Neutron service is extremely flexible, allowing operators to leverage different configurations and plugins. This flexibility is extremely powerful, but the tradeoff is that it can be difficult to identify and isolate problems as they arise. In this chapter, we will provide you with a method to make Neutron troubleshooting as painless as possible.

In this chapter, we will cover the following topics:

- Identifying Neutron issues
- Neutron services and agents
- Common problems
- Troubleshooting tools

Identifying Neutron issues

The first hurdle in resolving networking issues in OpenStack is learning how to identify these issues when you see them. There are some obvious signs of networking troubles, including the inability to ping one of your instances or the inability to access an instance via SSH. There are also some less-obvious signs that may not appear to be a networking issue at all, but as you troubleshoot, you may discover that networking is indeed the culprit.

Neutron services and agents

A properly running Neutron service will launch several Linux processes. When troubleshooting, you will want to make sure that all services are configured correctly and are running actively. If you run `pgrep -l neutron`, you should see a list of Neutron services, as shown in the following screenshot:

```
[root@ost-controller:~# pgrep -l neutron
20991 neutron-openvsw
21098 neutron-rootwra
21224 neutron-dhcp-ag
21333 neutron-l3-agen
21386 neutron-metadat
21419 neutron-metadat
21858 neutron-ns-meta
```

Depending on how you have deployed Neutron, the services listed in the preceding screenshot may be spread across multiple servers. For example, your neutron-server processes may be running on your controller node, all of the agents may be on your Network node, and your Compute nodes may also be running some of the agents.

To confirm that all the agents are running as expected, you can execute the neutron agent-list command. The output of this will look similar to what is shown in the following screenshot:

```
root@ost-controller:~# neutron agent-list
+-------------+-------------+------------+-------+----------------+-------------+
| id          | agent_type  | host       | alive | admin_state_up | binary      |
+-------------+-------------+------------+-------+----------------+-------------+
| 1a54cd63-a  | Open        | ost-       | :-)   | True           | neutron-ope |
| 609-469a-   | vSwitch     | controller |       |                | nvswitch-   |
| bc3d-bfc0c  | agent       |            |       |                | agent       |
| 2051544     |             |            |       |                |             |
| 43494b39-7  | DHCP agent  | ost-       | :-)   | True           | neutron-    |
| eb6-4272    |             | controller |       |                | dhcp-agent  |
| -91ad-ae54  |             |            |       |                |             |
| 24182337    |             |            |       |                |             |
| 5aa659af-1  | Metadata    | ost-       | :-)   | True           | neutron-    |
| c29-4212-b  | agent       | controller |       |                | metadata-   |
| f82-ea95e9  |             |            |       |                | agent       |
| 70c14e      |             |            |       |                |             |
| 5b8ce833    | L3 agent    | ost-       | :-)   | True           | neutron-l3- |
| -52fb-42ab  |             | controller |       |                | agent       |
| -a318-88ab  |             |            |       |                |             |
| c262d8ad    |             |            |       |                |             |
+-------------+-------------+------------+-------+----------------+-------------+
```

When the agent is up and running, the `alive` column will have `:-)`, and when the agent is not alive, the value will be xxx. If an agent is not alive and you are expecting it to be, you can attempt to start the agent. On Ubuntu, utilizing an Upstart script would be as simple as running `start neutron-openvswitch` or the equivalent of whichever agent you wanted to start. You can also attempt to start the agent manually by running the following command or the equivalent of the agent you are targeting:

```
sudo -u neutron neutron-openvswitch-agent --config-file=/etc/neutron/
neutron.conf --config-file=/etc/neutron/plugins/ml2/ml2_conf.ini --log-
file=/var/log/neutron/openvswitch-agent.log
```

Attempting to start the agent this way will allow you to see any errors that may be thrown on the startup, allowing you to troubleshoot agent startup issues.

Neutron logs

A good place to start is by having a look at the Neutron logs. By default, the neutron log files are located at the `/var/log/neutron/` directory. However, the log file location can be overridden. You can determine where Neutron is logging by looking at the Neutron processes. Run the `ps -aux | grep` command and look for the value in the `--log-file` attribute. You can also check the settings for `log_dir` in the `neutron.conf` file.

In the Neutron log directory, there should be several log files, one for the Neutron server, one for `neutron-ns-metadata-proxy`, and one for each of the agents. It's worth noting that if you do not see logs for a particular service, it may be a sign that the service hasn't started properly. The following is an example of what your neutron log directory might look like:

```
-rw-r--r-- 1 neutron neutron   1554 Feb 18 21:35 dhcp-agent.log
-rw-r--r-- 1 neutron neutron   2268 Feb 18 21:35 l3-agent.log
-rw-r--r-- 1 neutron neutron    492 Feb 18 21:35 metadata-agent.log
-rw-r--r-- 1 neutron neutron 225201 Feb 18 21:35 openvswitch-agent.log
-rw-r--r-- 1 neutron neutron   3982 Feb 18 21:35 server.log
```

It's good practice to check each log for errors, paying special attention to the timestamps. For example, we may start to examine the server.log file by running this:

```
less /var/log/neutron/server.log | grep ERROR
```

Execute this command for each file in the Neutron log directory and investigate each error in turn. You may also want to enable verbose logging when troubleshooting. To enable verbose logging for Neutron, you will want to set verbose to `True` in the `/etc/neutron/neutron.conf` file.

In the following section, we will work through some common networking problems, providing tips to identify and correct these issues.

Common problems

In this section, we will examine some of the common networking problems that you might face in an OpenStack cluster. We will provide steps to troubleshoot issues, and we will offer potential solutions to resolve the issue. It's worth repeating that there are multiple ways to configure Neutron, so the steps you take to solve the following issues may be slightly different depending on your installation. However, these steps should be useful to point you in the right direction.

When you can't ping an instance

If you have an active instance that you can't ping, there are a few things you want to check out. Working your way through the following steps should help you identify and correct the problem.

Security groups

Neutron uses security groups to control the access to instances. The access is controlled through IP filtering. Security groups are similar to `ip` tables rules of the instance. You can view a list of security groups by running this:

```
neutron security-group-list
```

On running this command, you will see a list of security groups in the system. Take the following code as an example:

```
root@ost-controller:~# neutron security-group-list
+----------------------------------+---------+------------------------------------+
| id                               | name    | security_group_rules               |
+----------------------------------+---------+------------------------------------+
| 1d4fa38b-                        | default | egress, IPv4                       |
| d4f4-4f32-a814-c8758ceca1f8      |         | egress, IPv6                       |
|                                  |         | ingress, IPv4, remote_group_id:    |
|                                  |         | 1d4fa38b-                          |
|                                  |         | d4f4-4f32-a814-c8758ceca1f8        |
|                                  |         | ingress, IPv6, remote_group_id:    |
|                                  |         | 1d4fa38b-                          |
|                                  |         | d4f4-4f32-a814-c8758ceca1f8        |
```

The preceding output prints each of the security groups and a summary of the rules under each security group. For example, in the rule listed previously, we see that instances in this security group have rules that allow egress on IPv4 and IPv6. You will also notice that the ingress rules for IPv4 and IPv6 refer to `remote_group_id`. The `remote_group_id` references the ID of a security group, and in this case, it is the same security group we are examining. This syntax is a shortcut that allows all instances in the security group indicated by `remote_group_id` to access the rule. So, in this case, all instances in the security group `1d4fa38b-d4f4-4f32-a814-c8758ceca1f8` will be allowed to receive ingress traffic from one another. If you spin up two or more instances in this security group, they will be able to pass traffic between each other.

To see a view of all the rules across all security groups, you can run the following command:

```
neutron security-group-rule-list
```

The output from this command will include all the rules from each of the security groups. This will allow you to see, at a `glance`, which rules are present for a given security group.

```
root@ost-controller:~# neutron security-group-rule-list
+---------------+---------------+-----------+-----------+---------------+-----------+
| id            | security_group | direction | ethertype | port/protocol | remote    |
+---------------+---------------+-----------+-----------+---------------+-----------+
| 02af5b35-dee  | default       | ingress   | IPv4      | any           | default   |
| 9-4df2-8167-  |               |           |           |               | (group)   |
| 75b83fd11911  |               |           |           |               |           |
| 075308de-4a3  | default       | ingress   | IPv4      | any           | default   |
| 2-4778-8596-  |               |           |           |               | (group)   |
| a3eee2fc2743  |               |           |           |               |           |
| 07d36f86-962  | default       | ingress   | IPv4      | any           | default   |
| 8-4f74-b066-  |               |           |           |               | (group)   |
| cb1aaf01f9ce  |               |           |           |               |           |
| 0a643965-e23  | default       | ingress   | IPv4      | any           | default   |
| 6-42c6-932e-  |               |           |           |               | (group)   |
| ec16d604d06c  |               |           |           |               |           |
```

Note that the default security group listed in the preceding output has rules for the ICMP protocol and the TCP protocol on port 22. These rules allow ping and SSH, respectively. You will also note that the remote value for the ping and SSH rules is set to 0.0.0.0/0. In this configuration, the ping and SSH request can come from any IP address on the network.

If you are having trouble pinging your instance or accessing it via SSH, make sure that the security group for the instance allows SSH on port 22 and icmp. For example, to allow your instance to be pinged from a machine outside the instances' security group, you can run the following nova command:

```
nova secgroup-add-rule default icmp -1 -1 0.0.0.0/0
```

The preceding command will add a rule to the default security group, allowing icmp traffic. The minimum and maximum ports are both set to -1, which will allow the ping to come over any port.

```
root@ost-controller:~# nova secgroup-add-rule default icmp -1 -1 0.0.0.0/0
+-------------+-----------+---------+------------+--------------+
| IP Protocol | From Port | To Port | IP Range   | Source Group |
+-------------+-----------+---------+------------+--------------+
| icmp        | -1        | -1      | 0.0.0.0/0  |              |
+-------------+-----------+---------+------------+--------------+
```

Once the rule has been added using the preceding nova command, you can confirm that it has been saved by running the list command again, as recorded in the following line of command:

```
neutron security-group-rule-list
```

This time, you should see the icmp rule returned in the output. Once the rule is present, you should be able to ping your instance, but there is one more concept that you need to be aware of. You may not be able to ping the instance using the standard syntax if your OpenStack installation is taking advantage of network namespaces.

Network namespaces

OpenStack allows the use of Network namespaces. When this feature is leveraged, it allows us to overlap IP addresses in different virtual networks. When this feature is active, you need to indicate which network namespace to use when trying to reach an instance. You can list the network namespaces in use by running this command:

```
ip netns list
```

This will return a list of namespaces that are active in your installation. Take the following output for example:

```
[root@ost-controller:~# ip netns list
qdhcp-7d3a9245-6837-4151-a0e2-6f5c9b50ee21
```

To ping an instance in this network namespace, you would run your command through the iproute2 exec command:

```
ip netns exec qdhcp-7d3a9245-6837-4151-a0e2-6f5c9b50ee21 ping 10.1.0.3
```

As you can see in the preceding command, you would use `ip` followed by the target, which is `netns` in our case. This stands for a network namespace. You would follow this by the action, which is `exec`, to execute a command in the namespace. Then, you would provide the name of the network namespace you are targeting followed by the command you wish to execute. In our case, we are attempting to ping our instance at `10.1.0.3`.

```
root@ost-controller:~# ip netns exec qdhcp-01d4125e-d1ba-43c5-9b92-9de7889
77bcd ping 10.1.0.3
PING 10.1.0.3 (10.1.0.3) 56(84) bytes of data.
64 bytes from 10.1.0.3: icmp_seq=1 ttl=64 time=1.31 ms
64 bytes from 10.1.0.3: icmp_seq=2 ttl=64 time=0.694 ms
```

In addition to using the `nova sec-group-add-rule` command, as we did in the preceding example, you can also use the neutron command-line client to add security group rules. For example, to add a security group rule that allows us to use SSH on our instances, we would run the following command:

```
neutron security-group-rule-create --direction ingress --ethertype IPv4
--protocol tcp --port-range-min 22 --port-range-max 22 --remote-ip-prefix
0.0.0.0/0 default
```

When using the neutron client, we pass in several attributes that set the characteristics of our rule. Upon successful creation, the preceding command will return the following output:

```
root@ost-controller:~# neutron security-group-rule-create --direction ingre
ss --ethertype IPv4 --protocol tcp --port-range-min 22 --port-range-max 22
--remote-ip-prefix 0.0.0.0/0 1d4fa38b-d4f4-4f32-a814-c8758ceca1f8
Created a new security_group_rule:
+--------------------+--------------------------------------+
| Field              | Value                                |
+--------------------+--------------------------------------+
| direction          | ingress                              |
| ethertype          | IPv4                                 |
| id                 | 48a11cde-7116-4875-bcf2-049383479f4e |
| port_range_max     | 22                                   |
| port_range_min     | 22                                   |
| protocol           | tcp                                  |
| remote_group_id    |                                      |
| remote_ip_prefix   | 0.0.0.0/0                            |
| security_group_id  | 1d4fa38b-d4f4-4f32-a814-c8758ceca1f8 |
| tenant_id          | a064ed4db59e4559be0fe2ad7d9a8ad0     |
+--------------------+--------------------------------------+
```

You can use the `neutron security-group-rule-list` command to confirm that the rule has been created. Once the rule is in place, you should be able to use SSH on your instance. Again, you will need to prefix your SSH call with the appropriate network namespace information. Take the following code as an example:

```
root@ost-controller:~# ip netns exec qdhcp-01d4125e-d1ba-43c5-9b92-9de78897
7bcd ssh cirros@10.1.0.3
```

You should be dropped into an SSH session for your instance, where you can log in as expected.

No IP address

When you spin up a new instance, you usually expect that instance to have an IP address. However, there are situations where your instance may become active without an assigned IP. Consider the following example for instance

```
+--------------------------------------+---------+--------+------------+-------------+----------+
| ID                                   | Name    | Status | Task State | Power State | Networks |
+--------------------------------------+---------+--------+------------+-------------+----------+
| 21978dfd-a356-47d5-a131-7927d38e0f82 | server2 | ACTIVE | -          | Running     |          |
+--------------------------------------+---------+--------+------------+-------------+----------+
```

The preceding example displays an instance that has the `Active` Status and a of `Running` Power State. You will also notice that the `Networks` column is empty. There are a few obvious things you want to check in this case.

The first thing you want to confirm is that there is a network available. To view a list of networks, you can run `neutron net-list`. If this command comes back empty, this means that you need to create a network and a subnetwork. We use the `neutron net-create` command to create a network. For example, to create a network named `private`, we would run the following command:

```
neutron net-create private
```

The output of this command will look similar to this:

```
root@ost-controller:~# neutron net-create private
Created a new network:
+----------------------------+--------------------------------------+
| Field                      | Value                                |
+----------------------------+--------------------------------------+
| admin_state_up             | True                                 |
| id                         | 9e83bddc-d597-4593-be98-0a5f36e62bc1 |
| mtu                        | 0                                    |
| name                       | private                              |
| provider:network_type      | gre                                  |
| provider:physical_network  |                                      |
| provider:segmentation_id   | 9                                    |
| router:external            | False                                |
| shared                     | False                                |
| status                     | ACTIVE                               |
| subnets                    |                                      |
| tenant_id                  | a064ed4db59e4559be0fe2ad7d9a8ad0     |
+----------------------------+--------------------------------------+
```

If you run the neutron net-list command again, you should now see the network you created.

```
root@ost-controller:~# neutron net-list
+--------------------------------------+---------+---------+
| id                                   | name    | subnets |
+--------------------------------------+---------+---------+
| 9e83bddc-d597-4593-be98-0a5f36e62bc1 | private |         |
+--------------------------------------+---------+---------+
```

While your new network should be present now, you will notice that the subnets column is blank. You will need to create a subnet that your instances can pull IP addresses from. To create a subnet, you need to leverage the `neutron subnet-create` command. Take the following code as an example:

```
neutron subnet-create --name private-subnet private 10.1.0.0/28
```

The preceding command creates a subnet named private-subnet. This subnet belongs to the network named private and uses a CIDR of 10.1.0.0./28. The output of the command is similar to the following output:

```
root@ost-controller:~# neutron subnet-create --name private-subnet private 10.1.0.0/28
Created a new subnet:
+-----------------------+----------------------------------------------------+
| Field                 | Value                                              |
+-----------------------+----------------------------------------------------+
| allocation_pools      | {"start": "10.1.0.2", "end": "10.1.0.14"}          |
| cidr                  | 10.1.0.0/28                                         |
| dns_nameservers       |                                                    |
| enable_dhcp           | True                                               |
| gateway_ip            | 10.1.0.1                                            |
| host_routes           |                                                    |
| id                    | 630a4164-ec1b-4445-aacc-00ba1250de6b               |
| ip_version            | 4                                                  |
| ipv6_address_mode     |                                                    |
| ipv6_ra_mode          |                                                    |
| name                  | private-subnet                                     |
| network_id            | 9e83bddc-d597-4593-be98-0a5f36e62bc1               |
| subnetpool_id         |                                                    |
| tenant_id             | a064ed4db59e4559be0fe2ad7d9a8ad0                   |
+-----------------------+----------------------------------------------------+
```

From the preceding output, you can see that the subnet has been created. DHCP is enabled on this network, and it belongs to the default tenant. Therefore, instances created on the default Tenant will receive an IP address from this subnet. You can confirm this by creating another server:

nova list

```
+--------------------------------------+---------+--------+------------+-------------+------------------+
| ID                                   | Name    | Status | Task State | Power State | Networks         |
+--------------------------------------+---------+--------+------------+-------------+------------------+
| 8c924f82-af36-43fd-bae0-c33b850fb3f1 | server1 | ACTIVE | -          | Running     | private=10.1.0.3 |
+--------------------------------------+---------+--------+------------+-------------+------------------+
```

This time, you will note that the instance has received an IP address from the network named private. If you have created appropriate security groups, you should be able to ping this IP from the DHCP namespace for this instance.

It is worth remembering that IP addresses are controlled by project-level quotas. Administrators can determine the size of the IP pool for each project. You can confirm the number of available floating IPs by checking the /etc/neutron/ neutron.conf file under the [QUOTAS] stanza. There, you may see a value for quota_floatingip, and that value represents the number of floating IPs per project. If this setting is not in your configuration file, then the value will be set to a default of 50. Users will need to return floating IPs to the pool before they can be used by other instances; otherwise, administrators can increase the floating IP quota.

Troubleshooting tools

Neutron is incredible, powerful, and extensible. It supports plugins for dozens of backends, but the two most commonly installed backends are Open vSwitch and Linux Bridge. As a result, you can take advantage of many of the common Linux troubleshooting tools when working with Neutron. In this section, we'll cover some of the basic Neutron troubleshooting tools, including `ovs-vsctl` and `iproute2`.

ovs-vsctl

This is used to configure and query Open vSwitch. This tool can be very useful when troubleshooting Neutron networks that leverage Open vSwith. For example, to see the contents of the configuration database, we can use the `ovs-vsctl show` command. Take the following example for instance:

```
root@ost-controller:~# ovs-vsctl show
f4c27671-284b-42c3-bf23-e95c26f78175
    Bridge br-tun
        fail_mode: secure
        Port patch-int
            Interface patch-int
                type: patch
                options: {peer=patch-tun}
        Port br-tun
            Interface br-tun
                type: internal
    Bridge br-int
        fail_mode: secure
        Port "qvo0208e670-ab"
            tag: 4095
            Interface "qvo0208e670-ab"
        Port "tapa4391bff-da"
            tag: 3
            Interface "tapa4391bff-da"
                type: internal
        Port br-int
            Interface br-int
                type: internal
        Port patch-tun
            Interface patch-tun
                type: patch
                options: {peer=patch-int}
        Port "qvo3f59c405-4c"
            tag: 4095
            Interface "qvo3f59c405-4c"
        Port "qvo194dbc44-1e"
            tag: 4095
            Interface "qvo194dbc44-1e"
        Port "qvo2321eced-29"
            tag: 3
            Interface "qvo2321eced-29"
    ovs_version: "2.0.2"
```

There are a few things worth pointing out in the preceding output. You'll notice that there are two bridges, one named br-int and another named br-tun. On br-int, there are multiple ports. There is one port named tapa4391bff-da. This is the tap interface coming from our instance. You will also notice a port with a name that begins with qvo...; this is one end of a **virtual Ethernet (veth)** pair connected to the OVS bridge. You want to make sure that these two ports are present:

iproute2

The IPRoute2 utility is a new collection to the tools that control TCP/IP traffic and networking in Linux. The iproute2 tools are designed to replace many of the legacy tools including ifconfig and route.

There are several useful commands included in this utility. For example, the IP link command will list out the networking devices on this host.

```
1: lo: <LOOPBACK,UP,LOWER_UP> mtu 65536 qdisc noqueue state UNKNOWN mode D
EFAULT group default
    link/loopback 00:00:00:00:00:00 brd 00:00:00:00:00:00
2: eth0: <BROADCAST,MULTICAST,UP,LOWER_UP> mtu 1500 qdisc pfifo_fast state
 UP mode DEFAULT group default qlen 1000
    link/ether bc:76:4e:20:7e:bd brd ff:ff:ff:ff:ff:ff
3: eth1: <BROADCAST,MULTICAST,UP,LOWER_UP> mtu 1500 qdisc pfifo_fast state
 UP mode DEFAULT group default qlen 1000
    link/ether bc:76:4e:21:16:fe brd ff:ff:ff:ff:ff:ff
```

In the preceding output, we see br-int and br-tun again. We also see the tap device. We also see a device that starts with qvo and another that starts with qvb. The letter q here refers to Quantum, which was the original name of the OpenStack Networking project before it was changed to Neutron. The letter v indicates that this device is one side of a veth pair. The letter b indicates the side of the veth pair that's plugged into the Linux bridge, and the letter o indicates the side of the veth pair that's plugged into the OVS switch.

The iproute2 has several other useful troubleshooting utilities, including ip route show, ip netns, and ip neigh.

The Neutron client

The Neutron command-line client also has several useful tools for research and troubleshooting. In addition to the commands we've seen so far, here are a few more useful ones.

The neutron port-list command allows you to see which ports have been created using neutron port-create. This output allows you to see the MAC address for each port as well as the IP address.

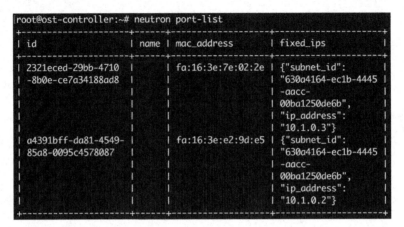

There are similar commands for routers, gateway devices, floating IPs, and more. Running the Neutron help command will give you the full list of the available tools.

Summary

OpenStack networking is very powerful with plenty of options. These options can make it difficult to troubleshoot. In this section, we gave you tips to troubleshoot some of the common Neutron problems and provided you with a list of tools to troubleshoot many others. Let's now dig into Nova.

5
Troubleshooting OpenStack Compute

Nova is one of the central services of OpenStack, and it is also one of the largest in terms of lines of code. It's also worth noting that Nova is one of the oldest OpenStack projects, and it has seen a lot of changes and development over the years. Nova leverages and interacts with many of the other OpenStack services. As a result, isolating and troubleshooting problems with Nova can be challenging, but in this chapter, we will give you the necessary tips to be successful.

When troubleshooting Nova, it helps to follow a series of steps as you seek to isolate the problems you may encounter. In this chapter, we will work through each of the following topics step by step as we troubleshoot Nova:

- Checking the services
- Checking the database
- Checking the authentication settings
- Checking the Glance integration
- Checking the Neutron integration

Checking the services

A successful Nova deployment will have multiple Nova services running, and, in addition, there will be multiple supporting services at play as well. A good first step when troubleshooting is to make sure that each of the services has been successfully initiated. We can check the various Nova services by running this command:

```
ps -aux | grep nova-
```

Be sure to include a dash (-), as the Nova services are prefixed with `nova-`. There are a lot of Nova processes, and in the following sections, we will look at each of these processes. The processes that we will explore are as follows:

- `nova-api`
- `nova-scheduler`
- `nova-conductor`
- `nova-compute`

nova-api

The Nova API service is usually run on the controller node. Nova supports an OpenStack API, which is the default, in addition to an AWS EC2 API. A request to port `8774` will be handled by the OpenStack API. A request to port `8773` will be handled by the AWS EC2 API. Nova also supports a metadata service, which will listen on port `8775`.

In order to confirm that the `nova-api` service is running, execute the following command:

```
ps -aux | grep nova-api
```

When `nova-api` is running as expected, the output from this command will look like the output shown here:

```
root@ost-controller:~# ps -aux | grep nova-api
root      11052  0.0  0.0  11980    920 pts/3     S+   21:29   0:00 grep nova
-api
nova      31751  0.5  3.2 244324 125800 ?         Ss   17:10   1:18 /usr/bin/
python /usr/local/bin/nova-api --config-file=/etc/nova/nova.conf
nova      31801  0.0  3.4 339136 134008 ?         S    17:10   0:00 /usr/bin/
python /usr/local/bin/nova-api --config-file=/etc/nova/nova.conf
nova      31802  0.0  3.4 338744 133940 ?         S    17:10   0:00 /usr/bin/
python /usr/local/bin/nova-api --config-file=/etc/nova/nova.conf
nova      31809  0.0  3.1 244324 121312 ?         S    17:10   0:00 /usr/bin/
python /usr/local/bin/nova-api --config-file=/etc/nova/nova.conf
nova      31810  0.0  3.1 244324 121312 ?         S    17:10   0:00 /usr/bin/
python /usr/local/bin/nova-api --config-file=/etc/nova/nova.conf
```

If the Nova API is not running, the preceding `ps -aux` command that you ran will come back with just the `grep` command and no `nova-api` processes. Also, when you attempt to use the command-line client with Nova, you may encounter an error like the following one:

```
Unable to establish connection to http://127.0.0.1:8774/v2/cc7343d7819a49f
7a01d5b699e894aeb/servers/detail
```

This is your first clue to any problems with the `nova-api` service. Your first course of action will be to attempt to start the `nova-api` service. On Ubuntu systems that use upstart, you can run this command:

```
start nova-api
```

Once you start the service, you should make sure that it has actually started and continues running successfully. At this point, you want to run `ps -aux | grep nova-api` again and make sure that the `nova-api` process is still up.

If the `nova-api` process isn't returned in the output, then I would recommend that you try to start the process manually. When you start an OpenStack process manually, that is, without the `init` scripts, any errors during startup will be printed to the console. If you are dealing with a process that fails on startup, your log files will most likely be empty. Starting the process manually will provide you with the clues that you need to troubleshoot further. To start the `nova-api` service manually, execute the following command:

```
sudo -u nova nova-api --config-file=/etc/nova/nova.conf
```

As the preceding command is executed, you will see the start up values printed to the console. Toward the end of this output, you will need to look for the lines indicating that your APIs have started up:

```
2016-02-17 21:42:43.289 21675 INFO nova.metadata.wsgi.server [-] (21675)
wsgi starting up on http://0.0.0.0:8775
2016-02-17 21:42:43.292 21676 INFO nova.metadata.wsgi.server [-] (21676)
wsgi starting up on http://0.0.0.0:8775
```

If you do not see lines similar to the lines shown in the preceding code snippet, you will most likely be staring at an error somewhere in the output. The good news is that this error will provide sufficient information to determine what is stopping the service from starting. While we cannot cover every potential cause within the confines of this book, we will take a look at the following few potential causes.

Address already in use

Suppose that, when starting the `nova-api` service manually, you see an error like the one shown here:

```
ERROR nova error: [Errno 98] Address already in use
```

This error means that there is something else running on port `8774`, which Nova uses for the API service. You can further troubleshoot this issue by running this command:

```
lsof -i :8774
```

This command will tell you what is running on port `8774`. Once you clear this port, you can attempt to start the `nova-api` service again by running `start nova-api`. As always, we want to check whether the `nova-api` process has started successfully by running the `ps -aux | grep nova-api` command. If the API has not started successfully, we can attempt to start it manually, as we did before, and look for the error output.

The permission error

Suppose that, when you attempt to start the `nova-api` process manually, you receive an error like the one shown here:

```
root@ost-controller:~# sudo -u nova nova-api --config-file=/etc/nova/nova.
conf
Traceback (most recent call last):
  File "/usr/local/bin/nova-api", line 10, in <module>
    sys.exit(main())
  File "/usr/local/lib/python2.7/dist-packages/nova/cmd/api.py", line 41,
in main
    config.parse_args(sys.argv)
  File "/usr/local/lib/python2.7/dist-packages/nova/config.py", line 59, i
n parse_args
    default_config_files=default_config_files)
  File "/usr/local/lib/python2.7/dist-packages/oslo_config/cfg.py", line 2
149, in __call__
    self._namespace._files_permission_denied)
oslo_config.cfg.ConfigFilesPermissionDeniedError: Failed to open some conf
ig files: /etc/nova/nova.conf
```

An error like the preceding one points to the fact that there is a permission or ownership problem with the Nova configuration file, typically located at /etc/ nova/nova.conf:

```
chmod 644 /etc/nova/nova.conf
```

```
chown nova:nova /etc/nova/nova.conf
```

The Nova configuration file needs to be readable by the Nova user. The preceding chmod and chown commands will set the proper permissions and ownership for this configuration file. After this fix, you can attempt to start the nova-api service again and verify that it is running successfully. If it doesn't start successfully, remember to check the nova-api.log file for clues.

nova-scheduler

The Nova scheduler service is responsible for selecting the compute node that will host a particular instance. If this service is not operating as expected, you will notice problems when trying to create new instances. To check whether the nova-scheduler service is running, we can use the following command:

```
ps -aux | grep nova-scheduler
```

The output of this command should have a line similar to the following one:

```
nova      32091  0.0  2.7 308540 104420 ?         Ss    Feb17    0:34 /usr/bin/
python /usr/local/bin/nova-scheduler --config-file=/etc/nova/nova.conf
```

If the Nova scheduler service does not start properly, there are a couple of things you should check. The first troubleshooting step should be attempting to start the nova-scheduler service manually. You can do this by running the following command:

```
 sudo -u nova /usr/bin/python /usr/local/bin/nova-scheduler --config-
file=/etc/nova/nova.conf
```

Any errors returned from this command should give you clues as to why the `nova-scheduler` service isn't starting. One error that you may see here is as follows:

```
root@ost-controller:~# sudo -u nova /usr/bin/python /usr/local/bin/nova-sc
heduler --config-file=/etc/nova/nova.conf
Traceback (most recent call last):
  File "/usr/local/bin/nova-scheduler", line 10, in <module>
    sys.exit(main())
  File "/usr/local/lib/python2.7/dist-packages/nova/cmd/scheduler.py", lin
e 36, in main
    config.parse_args(sys.argv)
  File "/usr/local/lib/python2.7/dist-packages/nova/config.py", line 59, i
n parse_args
    default_config_files=default_config_files)
  File "/usr/local/lib/python2.7/dist-packages/oslo_config/cfg.py", line 2
149, in __call__
    self._namespace._files_permission_denied)
oslo_config.cfg.ConfigFilesPermissionDeniedError: Failed to open some conf
ig files: /etc/nova/nova.conf
```

As we've seen before, the Nova configuration file located at `/etc/nova/nova.conf` needs to be readable by the Nova user. This error will cause problems with several Nova services, including the Nova scheduler. This problem can be resolved if you make sure that the configuration file is readable by the Nova user.

Once you run the `nova-scheduler` service successfully, you may still discover problems with the service. Your troubleshooting process should continue by looking at the `nova-scheduler` log for clues. The `nova-scheduler` log is typically located at `/etc/nova/nova-scheduler.log`. It is helpful to grep this log for errors by using a command like the one shown here:

```
less /var/log/nova/nova-scheduler.log | grep 'ERROR'
```

The output of this command will list any errors captured in the scheduler log files. There are a few errors to look out for in particular. To operate correctly, the Nova scheduler requires access to the OpenStack message broker and the Nova database.

```
2016-02-17 17:06:07.652 16404 ERROR oslo.messaging._drivers.impl_rabbit [-
] AMQP server on 127.0.0.1:5672 is unreachable: [Errno 111] ECONNREFUSED.
Trying again in 4 seconds.
```

The preceding error indicates that the `nova-scheduler` service is not able to connect to the AMQP server. In this instance, you want to make sure that the message broker is running and accessible. If you are using RabbitMQ, you can check its status by running this command:

```
rabbitmqctl status
```

When the RabbitMQ service is not running, the output of this command will look similar to the output shown here:

```
Status of node 'rabbit@ost-controller' ...
Error: unable to connect to node 'rabbit@ost-controller': nodedown

DIAGNOSTICS
===========

nodes in question: ['rabbit@ost-controller']

hosts, their running nodes and ports:
- ost-controller: [{rabbitmqctl11502,49424}]

current node details:
- node name: 'rabbitmqctl11502@ost-controller'
- home dir: /var/lib/rabbitmq
- cookie hash: hY/q1bh20AJifSDTJWP91A==
```

The fix for this problem is to start your message broker. For RabbitMQ, you can use the following command to start the message broker:

```
service rabbitmq-server start
```

You can confirm that RabbitMQ has started successfully by running the `rabbitmqctl status` command again. If RabbitMQ starts successfully, you will see an output similar to the following one:

```
[root@ost-controller:~# rabbitmqctl status
Status of node 'rabbit@ost-controller' ...
[{pid,17810},
 {running_applications,[{rabbit,"RabbitMQ","3.2.4"},
                        {os_mon,"CPO  CXC 138 46","2.2.14"},
                        {mnesia,"MNESIA  CXC 138 12","4.11"},
                        {xmerl,"XML parser","1.3.5"},
                        {sasl,"SASL  CXC 138 11","2.3.4"},
                        {stdlib,"ERTS  CXC 138 10","1.19.4"},
                        {kernel,"ERTS  CXC 138 10","2.16.4"}]},
 {os,{unix,linux}},
 {erlang_version,"Erlang R16B03 (erts-5.10.4) [source] [64-bit] [smp:2:2]
[async-threads:30] [kernel-poll:true]\n"},
 {memory,[{total,137752144},
          {connection_procs,1671584},
          {queue_procs,516360},
          {plugins,0},
          {other_proc,13285808},
          {mnesia,266872},
          {mgmt_db,0},
          {msg_index,40176},
          {other_ets,843344},
          {binary,99854640},
          {code,16522377},
          {atom,594537},
          {other_system,4156446}]},
 {vm_memory_high_watermark,0.4},
 {vm_memory_limit,1577284403},
 {disk_free_limit,50000000},
 {disk_free,45304135680},
 {file_descriptors,[{total_limit,924},
                    {total_used,41},
                    {sockets_limit,829},
                    {sockets_used,39}]},
 {processes,[{limit,1048576},{used,597}]},
 {run_queue,0},
 {uptime,61}]
...done.
```

In the `nova-scheduler.log` file, you should also see a confirmation that the scheduler was able to successfully connect to the message broker. Look for the log lines like the ones shown in this code snippet:

```
2015-09-27 23:52:28.248 2355 INFO oslo.messaging._drivers.impl_rabbit
[req-0c95b20c-a70d-40c8-bb90-deeec2f0cd47 - - - - -] Reconnected to AMQP
server on myrabbitserver:5672

2015-09-27 23:52:28.249 2355 INFO oslo.messaging._drivers.impl_rabbit
[req-0c95b20c-a70d-40c8-bb90-deeec2f0cd47 - - - - -] Connected to AMQP
server on myrabbitserver:5672
```

nova-compute

The Nova compute service needs to be running on each of the compute nodes. You can check whether the service is running by executing the following command:

```
ps -aux | grep nova-compute
```

If you find that the nova-compute service is not running, you can start the service by executing the following command on Ubuntu:

```
start nova-compute
```

After you attempt to start the nova-compute server, make sure that it is running successfully using the ps -aux command again. If the service does not start and remain running, you should try to start the service manually to check whether there are any errors printed out to the console. Use the following command to start the nova-compute service manually:

```
sudo -u nova nova-compute --config-file=/etc/nova/nova.conf --config-file=/etc/nova/nova-compute.conf
```

After executing this command, there will be several log lines containing the startup information for the service. You want to be on the look out for any errors or traces printed in this output. If something pops up, use the details of the error to troubleshoot further.

The compute service is responsible for interacting with the underlying hypervisor and plays a critical role when manipulating instances in OpenStack. If there are problems with the Nova compute service, this can result in multiple issues or errors. For example, if you attempt to launch a new instance without running the nova-compute service, you may see that the instance eventually ends up with an ERROR status. For example, when you run nova list, you may see an output like this:

```
root@ost-controller:~# nova list
+--------------------------------------+---------+--------+------------+-------------+----------+
| ID                                   | Name    | Status | Task State | Power State | Networks |
+--------------------------------------+---------+--------+------------+-------------+----------+
| 9240804b-c1ca-4107-bf63-358ab6934a54 | server1 | ERROR  | -          | NOSTATE     |          |
+--------------------------------------+---------+--------+------------+-------------+----------+
```

You will also notice that the status of the instance is ERROR. As demonstrated earlier, the first step is to make sure that the nova-compute service is running. If it is and you are still experiencing problems, there are several reasons why you may find your instance in this state. To find more clues about the root cause, we should begin looking through the Nova logs. When troubleshooting an instance with an ERROR state, you will want to look for errors in any of the following log files:

- /var/log/nova/nova-compute.log
- /var/log/nova/nova-scheduler.log
- /var/log/nova/nova-conductor.log

If the nova-compute service is indeed the root cause of the issue, you are likely to find an error in the nova-conductor.log command, similar to the error shown here:

```
Traceback (most recent call last):

  File "/usr/local/lib/python2.7/dist-packages/oslo_messaging/rpc/server.py
", line 150, in inner
    return func(*args, **kwargs)

  File "/usr/local/lib/python2.7/dist-packages/nova/scheduler/manager.py",
line 84, in select_destinations
    filter_properties)

  File "/usr/local/lib/python2.7/dist-packages/nova/scheduler/filter_schedu
ler.py", line 90, in select_destinations
    raise exception.NoValidHost(reason=reason)

NoValidHost: No valid host was found. There are not enough hosts available.
```

Remember that the nova-compute service is what abstracts the hypervisor in OpenStack. You can run the nova hypervisor-list command to see which hypervisors are available, and this can also give you clues about your compute hosts. For example, if we run nova hypervisor-list when the nova-compute service is down, we may see an output similar to this:

```
root@ost-controller:~# nova hypervisor-list
+----+---------------------+-------+---------+
| ID | Hypervisor hostname | State | Status  |
+----+---------------------+-------+---------+
| 1  | ost-controller      | down  | enabled |
+----+---------------------+-------+---------+
```

As you can see in this output, the state of the hypervisor is down. This would indicate that we need to look at the nova-compute service to ensure that it is functioning properly.

When the nova-compute service is running, but instances are still ending up with an error state, you can continue troubleshooting by looking at a few more potential causes.

```
2016-02-18 13:30:34.164 3945 ERROR nova.compute.manager [instance: 82f458ac
-dce4-4c5d-8059-91385add22a5] libvirtError: internal error: no supported ar
chitecture for os type 'hvm'
```

An error like the preceding one in the nova-compute.log file is an indication that you may have a configuration problem on your compute host. Specifically, this error points to the setting of virt_type in /etc/nova/nova-compute.conf. The fix here would be to change virt_type to a value accepted by your hypervisor. Specifically, we would change this value to qemu. Remember to restart the nova-compute service whenever you make a change to the nova-compute.conf configuration file.

nova-conductor

One of the purposes of the Nova conductor service is to handle all the database interactions on behalf of the compute nodes. This allows us to have a more secure installation, as the compute hosts don't have direct access to the database. To check whether nova-conductor is running, you can use the following command:

ps -aux | grep nova-conductor

If nova-conductor is running, the preceding command will return the following output:

```
[root@ost-controller:~# ps -aux | grep nova-conductor
nova       7845  0.5  2.4 213616 96096 ?          Ss   12:14   0:24 /usr/bin/p
ython /usr/local/bin/nova-conductor --config-file=/etc/nova/nova.conf
nova       7925  1.8  2.9 318904 113760 ?          S    12:14   1:29 /usr/bin/p
ython /usr/local/bin/nova-conductor --config-file=/etc/nova/nova.conf
nova       7926  1.8  2.9 318024 112912 ?          S    12:14   1:29 /usr/bin/p
ython /usr/local/bin/nova-conductor --config-file=/etc/nova/nova.conf
root       8168  0.0  0.0  11980   924 pts/2       S+   13:33   0:00 grep nova-
conductor
```

If the service is not running, you can start it by running a command similar to the following command:

```
start nova-conductor
```

Once you attempt to start the service, be sure to confirm that it is running successfully using the ps -aux command, like we did earlier. If you find that this service has not started in the right way, you should attempt to start the service manually and check the console for errors:

```
sudo -u nova nova-conductor --config-file=/etc/nova/nova.conf
```

When running the service manually, keep an eye on the console for traces or errors. These errors can help you identify issues that are prohibiting the Nova conductor from starting.

Since nova-compute has a dependency on nova-conductor, the order in which these services start is important. If you try to start nova-compute before nova-conductor, you will most likely see the following warning in your nova-compute.log file:

```
2016-02-18 13:38:16.269 11210 WARNING nova.conductor.api [req-c9d77643-3359
-4f72-8f4d-637f12260e24 - - - - -] Timed out waiting for nova-conductor.  I
s it running? Or did this service start before nova-conductor?  Reattemptin
g establishment of nova-conductor connection...
```

The fix for the preceding issue is to simply start nova-conductor and then start nova-compute. If your nova-conductor service is not running, you will have issues when trying to launch a new instance, as you can see in the following screenshot:

```
+--------------------------------------+---------+--------+------------+-------------+----------+
| ID                                   | Name    | Status | Task State | Power State | Networks |
+--------------------------------------+---------+--------+------------+-------------+----------+
| 848b0326-b3c9-457c-9faa-d2a22583172d | server2 | BUILD  | scheduling | NOSTATE     |          |
+--------------------------------------+---------+--------+------------+-------------+----------+
```

In the preceding example, the instance is stuck in the BUILD status with scheduling as the task state. A quick look at the nova-compute.log file will reveal the root of the issue, as shown in the following screenshot:

```
2016-02-18 13:45:16.311 11210 WARNING nova.conductor.api [req-c9d77643-3359
-4f72-8f4d-637f12260e24 - - - - -] Timed out waiting for nova-conductor.  I
s it running? Or did this service start before nova-conductor?  Reattemptin
g establishment of nova-conductor connection...
```

As the error message indicates that nova-conductor is not running. The fix here is to start the nova-conductor service. Nova can typically recover from this sort of error, allowing your instance to eventually build successfully:

Note that the status of the preceding instance is ACTIVE and the power state is Running. This indicates that the instance has been successfully created. While there are various issues that may cause an instance to build unsuccessfully, you can typically determine the root cause by following these points:

- Making sure that all the Nova services are running
- Checking the various Nova log files for clues

Supporting services

As you know, Nova works in concert with other OpenStack services, including Keystone, Glance, Neutron, and others. As a result, it is possible that problems with these services may manifest themselves as problems with Nova.

The Nova database

Nova makes use of a database to support its functionalities. If this database is not running or is improperly configured, it can cause your Nova installation to be unusable. To troubleshoot the Nova database, begin by making sure that the database engine is running. For example, when using MySQL, you can check the status by running the following command:

```
service mysql status
```

If the database is running, it will be indicated in the output of this command:

```
mysql start/running, process 15628
```

After confirming that the database engine is running, you should try to connect to the database server using the same parameters that are set up in the Nova configuration file. You can look up the connection information by running the following command:

```
less /etc/nova/nova.conf | grep "connection ="
```

The preceding command will search through the Nova configuration file, which is located at /etc/nova/nova.conf. In this file, we are looking for a variable named connection. This setting is typically under the stanza named [database]. The value of the variable will follow a format similar to the following format if you are using MySQL:

```
mysql://nova:novapwd@mydbserver/nova
```

From the preceding connection string, we see that our database server is running on the host named mydbserver with a database user named nova, and a password novapwd. We can use this information to attempt to connect to the database directly:

```
mysql -u nova -p -h mydbserver nova
```

On successful connection, a message similar to the one shown here will be printed on your console:

```
Welcome to the MySQL monitor.  Commands end with ; or \g.
Your MySQL connection id is 125
Server version: 5.5.47-0ubuntu0.14.04.1 (Ubuntu)

Copyright (c) 2000, 2015, Oracle and/or its affiliates. All rights reserved.

Oracle is a registered trademark of Oracle Corporation and/or its
affiliates. Other names may be trademarks of their respective
owners.

Type 'help;' or '\h' for help. Type '\c' to clear the current input statement.

mysql>
```

If the connection is unsuccessful, you will see a message like this one:

```
ERROR 1045 (28000): Access denied for user 'nova'@'localhost' (using password: YES)
```

This error indicates that we need to troubleshoot further. There are several possible causes behind this error. A few potential reasons include the following:

- Incorrect value for the database host
- Incorrect permission for users attempting to access the database
- Incorrect username and/or password

To troubleshoot further, you will need root access to the database server. Attempt to connect to the database using your root user. Accomplishing this step will also allow you to confirm the value for the database host:

```
mysql -u root -p -h mydbserver
```

Once you have logged into the database server as a root user, you will want to check the permissions for the Nova database user. An example of how to do this is included here:

```
show grants for 'nova'@'locahost'
```

The output of the preceding command will be similar to what is printed in the following screenshot:

```
mysql> show grants for 'nova'@'localhost';
+----------------------------------------------------------------------------------------------------+
| Grants for nova@localhost                                                                          |
+----------------------------------------------------------------------------------------------------+
| GRANT USAGE ON *.* TO 'nova'@'localhost' IDENTIFIED BY PASSWORD '*0BE3B501084D35F4C66DD3AC4569EAE5EA738212' |
| GRANT ALL PRIVILEGES ON `nova`.* TO 'nova'@'localhost'                                              |
+----------------------------------------------------------------------------------------------------+
2 rows in set (0.00 sec)
```

The nova user needs to be granted all permissions on the Nova database. After confirming that the nova user has the correct permissions, you want to make sure that the user's password is correct. You can change the nova user's password by executing the following set of commands:

```
1  mysql -u root -p
2  use mysql;
3  update user set password=PASSWORD('enter_new_password_here') where User='root';
4  flush privileges;
5  quit
```

After executing this series of commands, the password for the nova user will be updated. Make sure that this new value is properly reflected in the `connection` variable under the `[database]` stanza in the `/etc/nova/nova.conf` file.

After you have confirmed that your nova database user is set up correctly, you will want to make sure that the Nova database is properly initialized. The first step is to make sure that the Nova database exists. In MySQL, you can check this by running the following command:

```
show databases;
```

Make sure you see a database named nova in the list:

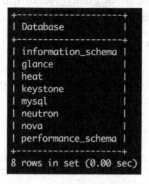

```
+--------------------+
| Database           |
+--------------------+
| information_schema |
| glance             |
| heat               |
| keystone           |
| mysql              |
| neutron            |
| nova               |
| performance_schema |
+--------------------+
8 rows in set (0.00 sec)
```

If the Nova database does not exist, you need to create it. You can do this using the standard SQL syntax. Take the following line of code as an example:

```
mysql> CREATE DATABASE nova;
```

Once you have confirmed that the database exists, you need to make sure that the required tables are present in the database:

```
mysql> show tables;
```

After running the preceding command, you will see list of tables in the Nova database. The following output is a partial list of tables. There are around 100 tables in total.

```
+------------------------------------------------+
| Tables_in_nova                                 |
+------------------------------------------------+
| agent_builds                                   |
| aggregate_hosts                                |
| aggregate_metadata                             |
| aggregates                                     |
| block_device_mapping                           |
| bw_usage_cache                                 |
| cells                                          |
| certificates                                   |
| compute_nodes                                  |
| console_pools                                  |
| consoles                                       |
| dns_domains                                    |
| fixed_ips                                      |
| floating_ips                                   |
```

When you run show tables and the command comes back empty, you will need to initialize your Nova database:

```
nova-manage db sync
```

The preceding command does not return an output, but it will create the necessary tables in the Nova database. Confirm this by running the show tables command again, after which you should see that your database is populated.

Nova authentication

The most obvious dependency Nova has is Keystone. Nova leverages Keystone to provide authentication services for all the Nova API calls. So, if Keystone is not running as expected, you will come to know this as soon as you attempt to use the OpenStack client:

```
openstack server list
```

If you try to use the preceding command to list the Nova servers while Keystone is not working, you will see an error like the one shown here:

```
Discovering versions from the identity service failed when creating the pas
sword plugin. Attempting to determine version from URL. Unable to establish
 connection to http://127.0.0.1:35357/v2.0/tokens
```

Keystone up

We will begin troubleshooting the integration between Nova and Keystone by making sure that Keystone is up and running:

```
ps -aux | grep keystone
```

This command should return an output similar to what is shown in the following screenshot:

```
root@ost-controller:~# ps -aux | grep keystone
keystone  3117  0.0  0.1 176300  5676 ?        Sl   15:54   0:00 (wsgi:keystone-pu -k start
keystone  3118  0.0  0.1 176300  5676 ?        Sl   15:54   0:00 (wsgi:keystone-pu -k start
keystone  3119  0.0  0.1 176300  5676 ?        Sl   15:54   0:00 (wsgi:keystone-pu -k start
keystone  3120  0.0  0.1 176308  5676 ?        Sl   15:54   0:00 (wsgi:keystone-pu -k start
keystone  3121  0.0  0.1 176300  5676 ?        Sl   15:54   0:00 (wsgi:keystone-pu -k start
keystone  3122  0.0  0.1 176308  5676 ?        Sl   15:54   0:00 (wsgi:keystone-ad -k start
keystone  3123  0.0  0.1 176300  5676 ?        Sl   15:54   0:00 (wsgi:keystone-ad -k start
keystone  3124  0.0  0.1 176300  5676 ?        Sl   15:54   0:00 (wsgi:keystone-ad -k start
keystone  3125  0.0  0.1 176300  5676 ?        Sl   15:54   0:00 (wsgi:keystone-ad -k start
keystone  3126  0.0  0.1 176300  5676 ?        Sl   15:54   0:00 (wsgi:keystone-ad -k start
```

If you do not see any Keystone processes running, refer to *Chapter 2, Troubleshooting OpenStack Identity*, in this book for Keystone troubleshooting tips.

Setting up the service user

Next, we will make sure that the Nova service user is set up correctly. By convention, this service user will be named `nova`. Confirm that this user exists by running the following command:

```
openstack user list
```

Running this command will return a list of users in Keystone. An example of the output is included in this screenshot:

Make sure that there is a user named `nova`. Secondly, this user should belong to a project/tenant named `service`, by convention. Make sure that the service project exists by running the following command:

```
openstack project list
```

This command will list the projects (tenants) configured in our Keystone installation:

In the output of this command, you should see a project named `service`, as demonstrated in the preceding screenshot. Next, we need to confirm that the `nova` user is assigned to the service project. We can accomplish this using the next command:

```
openstack user show nova
```

The preceding `user show` command will display details for the nova user as shown here:

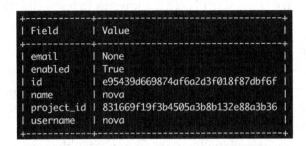

In the `project_id` field, we are looking for a project ID that matches the ID of our `service` project displayed in the preceding OpenStack project-list command. The project ID we are looking for is 831669f19f3b4505a3b8b132e88a3b36. The output tells us that our nova user is indeed a part of the `service` project.

Next, confirm that the nova user has the correct roles in Keystone. The following command can help us with that:

```
openstack user role list --project service nova
```

This command will list the roles for the glance user in the context of the service project:

```
+----------------------------------+----------+---------+------+
| ID                               | Name     | Project | User |
+----------------------------------+----------+---------+------+
| 9fe2ff9ee4384b1894a90878d3e92bab | _member_ | service | nova |
| 06ba482b2c3d43e382005dbff29e3608 | admin    | service | nova |
+----------------------------------+----------+---------+------+
```

Confirm that the nova user has the admin role in the service project.

Finally, confirm the password for the nova user. Use the OpenStack command-line client to authenticate as the nova user. Run a command similar to the one shown here:

```
openstack --os-username nova --os-password nova --os-project-name service
project list
```

The preceding command is the Openstack project list command, with a few arguments passed in on the command line. The arguments passed in will override the values we have in our `openrc` file. This allows us to test authentication with different users:

- `--os-username`: This indicates the username of the user we want to use. For this test, the username is `nova`.

- `--os-password`: This is the value we are targeting with this test. We want to make sure that the password is set and working as expected. For my test, I'm expecting the password to be `nova`.

- `--os-project-name`: Finally, we need to pass in the project name so that Keystone knows which project to authenticate under. Our user may have different roles under different projects. In our example, we are testing the `nova` user under the `service` project.

If the password for the `nova` user is equal to `nova`, as I expect, this command will return a list of projects in keystone, as follows:

```
+-------------------------------------------+---------+
| ID                                        | Name    |
+-------------------------------------------+---------+
| f075c50fafd242f59b3cdaaa827cd822          | demo    |
| 831669f19f3b4505a3b8b132e88a3b36          | service |
+-------------------------------------------+---------+
```

Suppose that I get an error like the one shown here:

```
The request you have made requires authentication. (HTTP 401) (Request-
ID: req-707fd197-ae15-4698-ac04-1de4c92acfe9)
```

This error tells me that the password is not `nova`, as I anticipated. At this point, I can try a few more password possibilities or I can reset the password. To reset the `nova` user's password, you can use a command like the one shown here:

```
openstack user set --password-prompt nova
```

After running this command, you will be prompted to enter a new password for the `nova` user. You will then be asked to type that password a second time to confirm it. After you reset the password, you can test it as we did earlier.

Finally, we need to confirm that our credentials are set properly in the Nova configuration files. In the /etc/nova/nova.conf file, there should be a keystone_ authtoken stanza. Under this stanza, make sure that the values of the admin_user and admin_password fields match with the values you have set in Keystone. Consider the following example:

```
1  [keystone_authtoken]
2  auth_uri = http://mykeystoneserver:5000
3  identity_uri = http://mykeystoneserver:35357/
4  admin_tenant_name = service
5  admin_user = nova
6  admin_password = nova
```

In the preceding example, admin_ user is set to nova and admin_password is set to nova. Replace these values with the username and password you have configured for your installation.

Service endpoints correct

At this stage, we should confirm that the service catalog contains the correct endpoints for the Nova service with the following command:

```
openstack endpoint show nova
```

When you run the endpoint show command, as demonstrated in the preceding code, you will see the details for the Nova endpoint in the service catalog. An example of a typical output is included in the following screenshot:

```
[root@ost-controller:~# openstack endpoint show nova
+--------------+-------------------------------------------+
| Field        | Value                                     |
+--------------+-------------------------------------------+
| adminurl     | http://127.0.0.1:8774/v2/$(tenant_id)s    |
| enabled      | True                                      |
| id           | 1ad909ed79cc4badb7832a88c56d0de9          |
| internalurl  | http://127.0.0.1:8774/v2/$(tenant_id)s    |
| publicurl    | http://127.0.0.1:8774/v2/$(tenant_id)s    |
| region       | RegionOne                                 |
| service_id   | 38fedbb8118d4f3aa2ef262d356c93af          |
| service_name | nova                                      |
| service_type | compute                                   |
+--------------+-------------------------------------------+
```

Confirm that the values of the `adminurl`, `internalurl`, and `publicurl` fields are correct. If any of these values are incorrect, you have the following three options to correct the issue:

- You can use the OpenStack `endpoint delete` command to remove the current endpoints, followed by the OpenStack `endpoint create` command.

- If you are using the default SQL driver for your service catalog, you can make the edits to the endpoints directly in the SQL database. Use caution when executing this option.

- If you are using the templated driver for your service catalog, you simply need to update your endpoint template file.

Nova and Glance

Nova depends on Glance when retrieving images while launching instances. If there is an issue that you're facing with Glance, you will most likely see it quickly when you attempt to launch a new instance using the `openstack server create` command:

```
openstack server create --flavor m1.tiny --image cirros-qcow2 server1
```

When this command is executed successfully, it will return a summary of the instance being created. If there is a problem with the Glance and Nova configurations, then you will see an error like the one shown here:

```
Could not find resource cirros-qcow2
```

If you run the same command with the `--debug` flag, you will see a more detailed error message like the one shown in the following screenshot:

```
Traceback (most recent call last):
  File "/usr/local/lib/python2.7/dist-packages/openstackclient/shell.py", l
ine 113, in run
    ret_val = super(OpenStackShell, self).run(argv)
  File "/usr/local/lib/python2.7/dist-packages/cliff/app.py", line 258, in
run
    result = self.run_subcommand(remainder)
  File "/usr/local/lib/python2.7/dist-packages/cliff/app.py", line 378, in
run_subcommand
    result = cmd.run(parsed_args)
  File "/usr/local/lib/python2.7/dist-packages/openstackclient/common/comma
nd.py", line 37, in run
    return super(Command, self).run(parsed_args)
  File "/usr/local/lib/python2.7/dist-packages/cliff/display.py", line 87,
in run
    column_names, data = self.take_action(parsed_args)
  File "/usr/local/lib/python2.7/dist-packages/openstackclient/compute/v2/s
erver.py", line 378, in take_action
    parsed_args.image,
  File "/usr/local/lib/python2.7/dist-packages/openstackclient/common/utils
.py", line 118, in find_resource
    raise exceptions.CommandError(msg)
CommandError: Could not find resource cirros-qcow2
```

This error clearly points to the fact that `glance-api` is not running or Glance is not configured correctly in the `nova.conf` file. The Glance configuration for Nova can be found under the `[glance]` stanza in `/etc/nova/nova.conf` as shown here:

```
1   [glance]
2   host = ip.of.glance.server
```

As demonstrated in the preceding code, you need to confirm the value of the `host` parameter for Glance. Once you confirm the Glance configuration in `nova.conf`, refer to *Chapter 3, Troubleshooting the OpenStack Image Service*, for more tips on Glance troubleshooting.

Nova and Neutron

Nova also depends on Neutron to provide networking for the instances. Nova will make API calls to Neutron after authenticating via Keystone. When attempting to launch an instance, you may come across and error like the one shown in the following screenshot:

```
Unexpected API Error. Please report this at http://bugs.launc
hpad.net/nova/ and attach the Nova API log if possible.
<class 'keystoneauth1.exceptions.connection.ConnectFailure'>
(HTTP 500) (Request-ID: req-2af322a9-cb94-44b3-9552-8380ade9d
de5)
```

Upon further troubleshooting, you may see errors in `nova-api.log` similar to the ones shown here:

```
2016-02-18 17:52:19.141 19155 ERROR nova.api.openstack.extensions ConnectFa
ilure: Unable to establish connection to http://127.0.0.1:9696/v2.0/floatin
gips.json?tenant_id=831669f19f3b4505a3b8b132e88a3b36
```

If you run across a similar error, make sure that the Neutron server is running and configured correctly in the `nova.conf` file.

```
1   [neutron]
2   auth_plugin = password
3   username = neutron
4   password = your_neutron_password
```

The preceding screenshot shows an example of the Neutron configuration in the nova. conf file. Make sure that this stanza exists, and the username and password values are correct for the Neutron service user. Once you have confirmed this, you can review the *Chapter 4, Troubleshooting OpenStack Networking*, for more tips.

Summary

Nova is a central service of OpenStack and is widely used. Understanding how to troubleshoot Nova effectively will go a long way. There are a lot of moving parts to Nova. However, you need to ensure that all the Nova services are running, the database is operating correctly, the Nova authentication setup is correct, Glance is configured properly, and Nova is configured properly. If you do all these accurately, you should be able to successfully navigate through most Nova troubleshooting issues. In the next chapter, we will dive into the world of OpenStack block storage as we look to troubleshoot Cinder.

6

Troubleshooting OpenStack
Block Storage

Cinder is the OpenStack service that provides persistent block storage for your Nova instances. Cinder block storage is like an external hard drive or USB drive for your instance, in that it can only be attached to one instance at a time. Cinder boasts a pluggable architecture, allowing OpenStack operators to leverage several backend storage plugins, for different types of storage. The supported plugins include Ceph, Sheepdog, NFS, Gluster, LVM, and others. While Cinder supports many storage drivers, we will focus on **Linux Volume Manager (LVM)**. In this chapter, we will cover the following topics:

- Troubleshooting Cinder processes
- Exploring Cinder logging
- Cinder authentication issues
- Cinder and RabbitMQ
- Common Cinder errors

Cinder processes

A working Cinder installation will have several processes running. Say, for example, you run the following command:

```
ps -aux | grep cinder
```

After this, you should see an output similar to the output shown here:

```
[root@ost-controller:~# ps -aux | grep cinder
cinder    2124  0.5  2.0 296132 79760 ?         Ss   18:03   0:22 /usr/bin/
python /usr/local/bin/cinder-api --config-file=/etc/cinder/cinder.conf --l
og-file=/var/log/cinder/api.log
cinder    2160  0.5  1.8 287024 72740 ?         Ss   18:03   0:22 /usr/bin/
python /usr/local/bin/cinder-volume --config-file=/etc/cinder/cinder.conf
--log-file=/var/log/cinder/volume.log
cinder    2177  0.0  2.1 303672 82532 ?         S    18:03   0:00 /usr/bin/
python /usr/local/bin/cinder-api --config-file=/etc/cinder/cinder.conf --l
og-file=/var/log/cinder/api.log
cinder    2178  1.7  2.2 307932 87016 ?         S    18:03   1:14 /usr/bin/
python /usr/local/bin/cinder-api --config-file=/etc/cinder/cinder.conf --l
og-file=/var/log/cinder/api.log
cinder    2190  1.9  1.9 295428 76668 ?         S    18:03   1:22 /usr/bin/
python /usr/local/bin/cinder-volume --config-file=/etc/cinder/cinder.conf
--log-file=/var/log/cinder/volume.log
cinder    2227  1.9  2.0 296208 79900 ?         Ss   18:03   1:23 /usr/bin/
python /usr/local/bin/cinder-scheduler --config-file=/etc/cinder/cinder.co
nf --log-file=/var/log/cinder/scheduler.log
root     11539  0.0  0.0  11984    920 pts/3    S+   19:15   0:00 grep cind
er
```

You will note that there are several `cinder-api` processes, several `cinder-volume` processes, and a `cinder-scheduler` process. When troubleshooting Cinder, you want to make sure that these three processes are up and successfully running. If one of the processes isn't running for some reason, you can use the respective `start` commands given here on Ubuntu systems using `upstart`:

```
start cinder-api
start cinder-volume
start cinder-scheduler
```

If you have trouble starting any of the processes using the `upstart` scripts, you may want to try and start them manually, where you will be able to see any errors that are being thrown on startup. To start the process manually, use the following command:

```
sudo -u cinder cinder-api --config-file=/etc/cinder/cinder.conf --log-
file=/var/log/cinder/cinder-api.log


sudo -u cinder cinder-scheduler --config-file=/etc/cinder/cinder.conf
--log-file=/var/log/cinder/cinder-scheduler.log


sudo -u cinder cinder-volume --config-file=/etc/cinder/cinder.conf --log-
file=/var/log/cinder/cinder-volume.log
```

It may also be helpful to double-check that the Cinder service is running correctly by executing the `service-list` command of Cinder:

```
cinder service-list
```

This command will output the status of the Cinder scheduler and volume service as displayed in the following screenshot:

```
root@ost-controller:~# cinder service-list
+------------------+----------------+------+---------+-------+------------
------------------+----------------+
|      Binary      |      Host      | Zone | Status  | State |        Upd
ated_at           | Disabled Reason |
+------------------+----------------+------+---------+-------+------------
------------------+----------------+
| cinder-scheduler | ost-controller | nova | enabled |  up   | 2016-02-25T
01:20:44.000000   |       -        |
|  cinder-volume   | ost-controller | nova | enabled |  up   | 2016-02-25T
01:20:43.000000   |       -        |
+------------------+----------------+------+---------+-------+------------
------------------+----------------+
```

You want to pay special attention to the `State` column for each process and make sure that it is `up`. If it isn't `up`, you can use the preceding methods that we've outlined to attempt to get it started.

Logging

It is worth pointing out that the log files for Cinder are typically located at `/var/log/cinder/`. In this directory, there will be log files for the API, the volume and scheduler service of Cinder. If you have trouble getting any of the Cinder process to start, you may want to check the logs for any clues. You may find it helpful to grep the logs for errors using a command similar to the one given here:

```
less /var/log/cinder/volume.log | grep ERROR
```

This command will allow you to see all of the error lines in the volume log file. Running the command is a very quick way to locate errors in the logs and identify clues that might help you resolve the issue.

Cinder dependencies

Like most other OpenStack services, Cinder has dependencies on other OpenStack components. These components must be present and operate successfully in order for Cinder to do its job. In a troubleshooting scenario, you want to check these dependencies and confirm that they are up and running.

Keystone authentication problems

Cinder leverages Keystone to provide authentication and authorization services. If the Keystone service is not running, it shouldn't take long for you to see the result. If you run a `cinder` command, such as `cinder list` or `cinder create` without running Keystone, you will see an error like the one shown here:

```
ERROR: Unable to establish connection to http://127.0.0.1:35357/v2.0/tokens
```

In this case, you want to check and make sure that the Keystone service is up and running. Refer to *Chapter 2, Troubleshooting OpenStack Identity*, for details on how to make sure that Keystone is running successfully. Imagine a scenario where you have confirmed that Keystone is up and running and yet when you run a `cinder` command you receive an error similar to the following:

```
ERROR: Service Unavailable (HTTP 503)
```

In this case, you want to check the Cinder API log at `/var/log/cinder/api.log`. You are looking for a `CRITICAL` line or `INFO` line like the ones shown here:

```
2016-02-24 19:55:40.863 16822 WARNING keystonemiddleware.auth_token [-]
Identity response: {"error": {"message": "Invalid user / password (Disab
le debug mode to suppress these details.)", "code": 401, "title": "Unaut
horized"}}
2016-02-24 19:55:40.864 16822 CRITICAL keystonemiddleware.auth_token [-]
 Unable to validate token: Identity server rejected authorization necess
ary to fetch token data
```

The preceding error provides a clue that there is a problem with the authorization credentials that are used to fetch the `auth` token. In this case, you want to double-check the password of the `cinder` user as indicated in `/etc/cinder/cinder.conf`. Make sure that the credentials match the values loaded in Keystone for that user.

RabbitMQ problems

Cinder makes use of an AMQP server, which is typically provided by RabbitMQ in OpenStack installations. You want to confirm that RabbitMQ is up and running correctly. Suppose that you attempt to run a `cinder create` command such as this:

```
cinder create --name MyVol 1
```

If the preceding command hangs with no output, then check your `Cinder api` log at `/var/log/cinder/api.log`:

```
2016-02-24 20:03:46.922 17897 ERROR oslo.messaging._drivers.impl_rabbit
[req-2c36d609-adee-4879-bc71-907de92a6dfd - - - - -] AMQP server on 127.
0.0.1:5672 is unreachable: [Errno 111] ECONNREFUSED. Trying again in 4 s
econds.
```

The preceding error is an example of what you will see when Cinder is unable to connect to your message broker. Cinder will keep trying to reconnect, and you will likely see a series of similar log lines in `api.log`. In this case, confirm that your AMQP server is up and running at the location indicated at `/etc/cinder/cinder.conf`.

Cinder errors

In this section, we will explore a few of the more common errors you might encounter with Cinder. While we highlight just a few of the errors you may come across, the troubleshooting techniques we illustrate should be helpful in various troubleshooting situations.

Missing the cinder-volumes volume group

When using **LVM** to back Cinder, OpenStack expects there to be a volume group named `cinder-volumes`. When running the `vgdisplay` command, you can check for the `cinder-volumes` volume group as shown here:

```
[root@ost-controller:~# vgdisplay
  --- Volume group ---
  VG Name               cinder-volumes
  System ID
  Format                lvm2
  Metadata Areas        1
  Metadata Sequence No  2
  VG Access             read/write
  VG Status             resizable
  MAX LV                0
  Cur LV                1
  Open LV               0
  Max PV                0
  Cur PV                1
  Act PV                1
  VG Size               8.00 GiB
  PE Size               4.00 MiB
  Total PE              2047
  Alloc PE / Size       256 / 1.00 GiB
  Free  PE / Size       1791 / 7.00 GiB
  VG UUID               nGtzLy-BKQu-WYMV-J7T5-KxXx-elwQ-nU1RJg
```

If you attempt to create cinder volume without having a volume group named `cinder-volumes`, it's very likely that your volume will end up in an error state as illustrated in the following screenshot with `MyVol2`:

```
root@ost-controller:~# cinder list
+--------------------------------------------------+-------------+-----------------+--
--------+------+-------------+----------+-----------+--------------+
|                     ID                           |   Status    | Migration Status |
  Name  | Size | Volume Type | Bootable | Multiattach | Attached to |
+--------------------------------------------------+-------------+-----------------+--
--------+------+-------------+----------+-----------+--------------+
| 3f177530-920e-4952-af4d-7c3f2eb3db42 | available |      -      |
MyVol1 |  1   |      -      |  false   |    False    |             |
| 477ab225-115c-4248-b085-fd8a0f366994 |   error   |      -      |
MyVol2 |  2   |      -      |  false   |    False    |             |
+--------------------------------------------------+-------------+-----------------+--
--------+------+-------------+----------+-----------+--------------+
```

You can further confirm that this is the issue by checking the scheduler log at `/var/log/cinder/scheduler.log file`. In this log file, you are looking for an error similar to the one shown here:

```
c-4248-b085-fd8a0f366994 cinder-volumes -L 2g\nExit code: 5\nStdout: u\'\'
\nStderr: u\'  Volume group "cinder-volumes" not found\\n\'\n']
```

The last line in the log file may point to the fact that `No valid host was found`, but if you look further up in the log, you will note the logline that says `Volume group cinder-volumes not found`. This is a clue that points to the fact that you are missing a volume group named `cinder-volumes`. To resolve this issue, you can rename your volume group by running `vgrename` as in the following example:

```
vgrename my-volumes cinder-volumes
```

You can confirm the rename by running `vgdisplay` again and make sure that the value of the `VG Name` line is `cinder-volumes`.

The volume stuck in the creating state

At some point, you may find yourself in a situation where you have a Cinder volume stuck in the `creating` state. An example of this is the last volume in the following output:

```
root@ost-controller:~# cinder list
+--------------------------------------------+-----------+-----------------+
+--------+------+-------------+-----------+-----------+--------------+
|                    ID                      |  Status   | Migration Status |
|  Name  | Size | Volume Type | Bootable | Multiattach | Attached to |
+--------------------------------------------+-----------+-----------------+
+--------+------+-------------+-----------+-----------+--------------+
| 87395813-5d5d-4587-a708-8bff4e5c9daf | creating |        -        |
| MyVolA | 1    |      -      |  false   |   False   |              |
+--------------------------------------------+-----------+-----------------+
+--------+------+-------------+-----------+-----------+--------------+
```

The problem with having a volume stuck in the `creating` state is that Cinder will not let you delete it. When you attempt to delete a volume in this state, you will receive an error similar to the one given here:

Delete for volume 87395813-5d5d-4587-a708-8bff4e5c9daf **failed: Invalid volume: Volume status must be available or error, but current status is: creating. (HTTP 400) (Request-ID: req-20d4120a-9c91-466b-8e6b-f0b76f4356de)**

ERROR: Unable to delete any of the specified volumes.

As illustrated in the preceding error, Cinder will not let you delete a volume unless it is in the `Available` or `Error` state. To fix this issue, you can run the `cinder reset-state` command:

cinder reset-state 87395813-5d5d-4587-a708-8bff4e5c9daf

After running this command, the volume will be moved to the `available` or `error` state, after which you can use the `delete` command to remove the volume if it's in `error`, or you can attach the volume if it's `available`. Make sure that the ID passed into this command matches the ID of the volume you are targeting. This command changes the status of the volume in the database, so you need to make sure that the Cinder database is initialized and running as expected.

Insufficient free space

If you attempt to create a volume only to be confronted with an error similar to the one here, then you may want to check a few things:

Volume group "cinder-volumes" has insufficient free space

If you are using LVM, then you can run `vgdisplay` to confirm the volume group size you are working with. If necessary, you can use `vgextend` to increase the size of the volume group.

Not sending heartbeat

Suppose that during your troubleshooting, you come across a series of errors in the /var/log/cinder/volume.log file similar to the one given here:

```
2015-10-19 05:01:38.492 2499 ERROR cinder.service [-] Manager for service
cinder-volume tc-ost1 is reporting problems, not sending heartbeat.
Service will appear "down".
```

This error indicates that Cinder may not be running properly. To further troubleshoot the problem, look at the log entries that have been recorded just before the heartbeat errors appear. Here, you will likely find clues pointing to the cause of the root issue.

Summary

Cinder provides a persistent block storage service for OpenStack. The service is not overly complex, but there are a few things that can cause it to break. There will likely come a time when you need to troubleshoot Cinder. In this chapter, you learned how to troubleshoot the Cinder processes, check the log files, and confirm the authentication settings. We also looked at how to troubleshoot Cinder and RabbitMQ, and finally, we looked at some common Cinder errors. With the tools and tips presented in this chapter, you should be well on your way to solving the common Cinder issues that come your way. In the following chapter, we will work with Swift, OpenStack's object storage.

7
Troubleshooting OpenStack Object Storage

In this chapter, we will examine some of the common troubleshooting scenarios you may encounter when working with OpenStack object storage, otherwise known as Swift. In the last chapter, you learned about troubleshooting OpenStack block storage. In this chapter, we will explore object storage. Access to data in object storage is achieved through an API as opposed to direct filesystem access; that is, object storage is not a hard drive. As a result, our troubleshooting techniques will not follow the typical troubleshooting techniques that are used when troubleshooting block storage. However, there are some things that you need not worry much about with Swift object storage. The system is designed to store your data durably. Swift is designed to expect failure, which also makes a properly configured installation extremely durable. The topics we will cover in this chapter are as follows:

- Troubleshooting Swift processes
- Troubleshooting Swift authentication, including:
    ◦ TempAuth
    ◦ Swauth
    ◦ Keystone

Swift processes

Swift spawns several processes. When troubleshooting, you will want to confirm that each process is running without any issue. In particular, you want to confirm that the main processes are active and running as expected. The following are the names of the main processes:

- The proxy server
- The account server
- The container server
- The object server

The proxy server

The Swift proxy server acts as a gateway to the service. The proxy server is where the Swift API listens for requests. There are several errors that may point to the fact that the Swift proxy server isn't running. The `swift list` command will list the containers under an account. In the following example, instead of returning a list of containers, this command returned an error:

```
root@ost-swift:~# swift list
HTTPConnectionPool(host='127.0.0.1', port=8080): Max retries exceeded with
  url: /v1/AUTH_81dba8100de14e7d86ddbf3bb3a009ee?format=json (Caused by New
ConnectionError('<requests.packages.urllib3.connection.HTTPConnection obje
ct at 0x7fb455f47090>: Failed to establish a new connection: [Errno 111] C
onnection refused',))
```

The preceding connection error is an example of what you might see when attempting to use the Swift command-line tool when the proxy server is not running. If you attempt to use the Swift API when the proxy server is in this state, you are likely to see an error similar to the one shown here:

```
root@ost-swift:~# curl -v -H 'X-Storage-User: test:tester' -H 'X-Storage-P
ass: testing' http://127.0.0.1:8080/auth/v1.0
* Hostname was NOT found in DNS cache
*   Trying 127.0.0.1...
* connect to 127.0.0.1 port 8080 failed: Connection refused
* Failed to connect to 127.0.0.1 port 8080: Connection refused
* Closing connection 0
curl: (7) Failed to connect to 127.0.0.1 port 8080: Connection refused
```

The quickest way to resolve this is by starting the `proxy-server` service. You can do this by using the `swift-init` tool:

```
swift-init main start
```

Swift authentication

One of the unique characteristics of Swift, when compared to other OpenStack projects is that Swift can be run completely standalone. While Swift can be used with other OpenStack projects, it does not have any direct dependencies on those projects. For example, Swift can be configured to use its own internal authentication system or it can be configured to use Keystone. It is important to understand this nuance when troubleshooting Swift Authentication problems. Typically, a Swift installation will be configured to use one of the three authentication methods: TempAuth, Swauth, or Keystone. To determine which authentication method Swift is using, look in the `proxy-server.conf` configuration file located at `/etc/swift/proxy-server.conf`. In this file, there is a stanza named `[pipeline:main]`. This stanza will contain a string representing the authentication method being used, either `tempauth` or `swauth`.

Troubleshooting TempAuth

TempAuth, as the name implies, is a temporary authorization system designed to get you up and running quickly with Swift. This authentication option allows you to test Swift, but it is not intended for production deployments. Most of the configuration for TempAuth will be done in the `proxy-server.conf` file, including the usernames and passwords to be used with TempAuth.

TempAuth configuration

When troubleshooting TempAuth, the first thing you want to do is confirm that you are running TempAuth:

```
1   [pipeline:main]
2   # Yes, proxy-logging appears twice. This is so that
3   # middleware-originated requests get logged too.
4   pipeline = catch_errors gatekeeper healthcheck
5   proxy-logging cache bulk tempurl ratelimit crossdomain
6   container_sync tempauth staticweb container-quotas
7   account-quotas slo dlo versioned_writes proxy-logging
8   proxy-server
```

As illustrated in the preceding code snippet, in the `[pipeline:main]` section of `proxy-server.conf`, there will be a `tempauth` entry in the pipeline if TempAuth is in use. If your deployment is using TempAuth and you are troubleshooting `auth` problems, you'll want to check the rest of the TempAuth configuration.

In addition to the `tempauth` entry in the pipeline, there should be the `tempauth` filter section, similar to the one displayed here:

```
1  [filter:tempauth]
2  use = egg:swift#tempauth
3  user_admin_admin = admin .admin .reseller_admin
4  user_test_tester = testing .admin
5  user_test2_tester2 = testing2 .admin
6  user_test_tester3 = testing3
```

Lines 3-6 in the preceding output define the various users' setup to work with TempAuth. In the preceding example, the user entries follow this format:

```
User_<account>_<username> = <password> [.<role>]
```

When attempting to make calls to Swift via the API, the credentials used should match the values in the `[filter:tempauth]` section of your configuration file:

```
curl -v -H 'X-Storage-User: test:tester' -H 'X-Storage-Pass: testing'
http://swiftproxyserver:8080/auth/v1.0
```

As demonstrated in the preceding lines of code, you will pass in `<account>:<username>` into the `X-Storage-User` header. In our example, we are using the `tester` user under the `test` account. If everything works as expected, the output from this `curl` call will be similar to the output shown here:

```
root@ost-swift:~# curl -v -H 'X-Storage-User: test:tester' -H 'X-Storage-
Pass: testing' http://127.0.0.1:8080/auth/v1.0
* Hostname was NOT found in DNS cache
*   Trying 127.0.0.1...
* Connected to 127.0.0.1 (127.0.0.1) port 8080 (#0)
> GET /auth/v1.0 HTTP/1.1
> User-Agent: curl/7.35.0
> Host: 127.0.0.1:8080
> Accept: */*
> X-Storage-User: test:tester
> X-Storage-Pass: testing
>
< HTTP/1.1 200 OK
< X-Storage-Url: http://127.0.0.1:8080/v1/AUTH_test
< X-Auth-Token: AUTH_tka598de20d6d74085825eacaf0355e67e
< Content-Type: text/html; charset=UTF-8
< X-Storage-Token: AUTH_tka598de20d6d74085825eacaf0355e67e
< Content-Length: 0
< X-Trans-Id: tx3782358c7fb44d79a1429-0056ca4c9d
< Date: Sun, 21 Feb 2016 23:47:41 GMT
<
* Connection #0 to host 127.0.0.1 left intact
```

You can test Swift by attempting to run GET on the account. To do this, you need to use X-AUTH-Token that was returned in the preceding call as well as X-Storage-Url. With these two values in hand, you can run a curl command similar to the following one:

```
curl -v -H 'X-Auth-Token: AUTH_tk8c7ae187154749ccb121397f6779f11e'
http://127.0.0.1:8080/v1/AUTH_test
```

The preceding curl command will return an output similar to the output shown in the following screenshot:

```
root@ost-swift:~# curl -v -H 'X-Auth-Token: AUTH_tka598de20d6d74085825eaca
f0355e67e' http://127.0.0.1:8080/v1/AUTH_test
* Hostname was NOT found in DNS cache
*   Trying 127.0.0.1...
* Connected to 127.0.0.1 (127.0.0.1) port 8080 (#0)
> GET /v1/AUTH_test HTTP/1.1
> User-Agent: curl/7.35.0
> Host: 127.0.0.1:8080
> Accept: */*
> X-Auth-Token: AUTH_tka598de20d6d74085825eacaf0355e67e
>
< HTTP/1.1 204 No Content
< Content-Type: text/plain; charset=utf-8
< X-Account-Object-Count: 0
< X-Timestamp: 1456098652.29311
< X-Account-Bytes-Used: 0
< X-Account-Container-Count: 0
< X-Put-Timestamp: 1456098652.29311
< Content-Length: 0
< X-Trans-Id: tx18487eb03cd840bf8285e-0056ca4d5c
< Date: Sun, 21 Feb 2016 23:50:52 GMT
<
* Connection #0 to host 127.0.0.1 left intact
```

We have executed this command against an empty Swift cluster, but it's worth noting the statistics that are returned from this call. X-Account-Object-Count lists the number of objects in this account. The X-Account-Container-Count list displays the number of containers in the account. The X-Account-Bytes-Used command shows the number of bytes used in this account.

If there is a problem with the credentials, you will see an error similar to the following one when you run `curl`:

```
* Hostname was NOT found in DNS cache
*    Trying 127.0.0.1...
* Connected to 127.0.0.1 (127.0.0.1) port 8080 (#0)
> GET /v1/AUTH_test HTTP/1.1
> User-Agent: curl/7.35.0
> Host: 127.0.0.1:8080
> Accept: */*
> X-Auth-Token: AUTH_tk8c7ae187154749ccb121397f6779f11e
>
< HTTP/1.1 401 Unauthorized
< Content-Length: 131
< Content-Type: text/html; charset=UTF-8
< Www-Authenticate: Swift realm="AUTH_test"
< X-Trans-Id: txdd0c450ba4134d2387ec7-0056ca4dd5
< Date: Sun, 21 Feb 2016 23:52:53 GMT
<
* Connection #0 to host 127.0.0.1 left intact
<html><h1>Unauthorized</h1><p>This server could not verify that you are au
thorized to access the document you requested.</p></html>root@ost-swift:~#
```

Take a note of the `401 Unauthorized` error returned from this call. In addition to this, the body returned includes a message explaining that the user's authorization could not be verified. These errors point to the fact that one of the credentials used in the `curl` call was incorrect. To resolve this issue, verify the credentials set at `/etc/swift/proxy-server.conf` against the credentials used in the `curl` call.

For users who utilize the Swift command-line tool, you will typically use a syntax similar to the following syntax:

```
swift -U test:tester -K testing -A http://127.0.0.1:8080/auth/v1.0/ auth
```

When this command is executed successfully, you will see an output similar to the one shown here:

```
[root@ost-swift:~# swift -U test:tester -K testing -A http://127.0.0.1:8080]
/auth/v1.0/ auth
export OS_STORAGE_URL=http://127.0.0.1:8080/v1/AUTH_test
export OS_AUTH_TOKEN=AUTH_tka598de20d6d74085825eacaf0355e67e
```

Note that the pattern of the user (`-U`) attribute is `<account>:<username>`. Suppose that, when you attempt to use the Swift command-line tool with TempAuth, you come across an error similar to the following one:

```
Auth GET failed: http://127.0.0.1:8080/auth/v1.0/ 401 Unauthorized
```

There are a few settings that you need to check when you come across a 401 Unauthorized error when using the Swift command-line tool. To troubleshoot this error, you need to check the account, username, password, and auth URL being used.

The account and username

When using the Swift command-line tool, you need to pass in the account and the username for the user you are authenticating. For example, to run the Swift list command with authentication arguments passed in on the command line, you would use the following code:

```
[root@ost-swift:~# swift -A http://127.0.0.1:8080/auth/v1.0 -U test:tester
-K testing list
sample_container
```

The tool expects user information to be passed as <Account>:<Username>. For example, for an account named test and a username tester, the value passed to the -U argument of the Swift tool would be test:tester. If you omit the account value, you are likely to see the preceding 401 Unauthorized error.

You can pass the account and username as an argument into the Swift tool or you can set these values in an environment variable named ST_USER, as demonstrated in line **2** of the following screenshot:

```
1   export ST_AUTH=http://127.0.0.1:8080/auth/v1.0
2   export ST_USER=test:tester
3   export ST_KEY=testing
```

These values may be added to a swiftrc file or you can include them in the openrc file along with the environment variables for other OpenStack services. When troubleshooting the Swift tool with TempAuth, be sure to check for the Swift tool environment variables, ST_AUTH, ST_USER, and ST_KEY, and if they are being used, make sure they are correct. It may also be helpful to unset these environment variables while troubleshooting and pass the values explicitly. The values passed into the Swift tool should match those set in the [filter:tempauth] section of the /etc/swift/proxy-server.conf file.

The password

The Swift command-line tool also requires a password for the user you are authenticating as. The password can be passed in as the key (-K) attribute or it can be set in the ST_KEY environment variable. Refer to the preceding screenshot for an example. An incorrect password will also cause a 401 Unauthorized error. Make sure that the value being passed into the Swift tool matches the value in the [filter:tempauth] section of the /etc/swift/proxy-server.conf file.

400 Bad Request

If you receive a `400 Bad Request` error when attempting to use the Swift tool with TempAuth, it may indicate that you have configured an incorrect Auth URL. The error may look similar to the one given here:

```
Auth GET failed: http://127.0.0.1:8080/auth2/v1.0 400 Bad Request
```

If you receive this error, then you want to confirm that the value is being passed into the `auth` (`-A`) parameter of the Swift command-line tool. This value may also be set as the `ST_AUTH` environment variable. The value set in the `ST_AUTH` environment variable and any value passed into the `-A` argument of the Swift tool should match the value in the `[filter:tempauth]` section of the `/etc/swift/proxy-server.conf` file.

Troubleshooting Swauth

Operators of Swift that are looking to move past TempAuth and leverage something a little more production ready might opt to use Swauth instead, which is a Swift authentication system. One of the unique characteristics of Swauth is that it uses the Swift cluster to store the authentication credentials much in the same way as standard objects are stored in the cluster.

You can confirm that your deployment is configured to use Swauth by checking the pipeline setting in `/etc/swift/proxy-server.conf`:

```
1   ## Swauth Pipeline
2   pipeline = catch_errors gatekeeper
3   healthcheck proxy-logging cache container_sync
4   bulk tempurl ratelimit container-quotas
5   account-quotas slo dlo versioned_writes
6   proxy-logging swauth proxy-server
```

If there is a `swauth` entry in the pipeline and a `[filter:swauth]` section, like the one shown here, then your deployment is configured to use Swauth:

```
1   [filter:swauth]
2   use = egg:swauth#swauth
3   set log_name = swauth
4   super_admin_key = swauthkey
5   default_swift_cluster = local#http://127.0.01:8080/v1
```

When attempting to start or restart the proxy server, if you come across a trace that ends with a line similar to the one given here, then this is a sign that your installation doesn't have the `swauth` package installed:

```
pkg_resources.DistributionNotFound: The 'swauth' distribution was not
found and is required by the application
```

To correct this problem, simply install the `swauth` packages using the package manager for your distribution. This package needs to be installed on every server running the `swift-proxy` service.

Swauth initialization

If you are having trouble using Swauth, you should confirm that Swauth has been successfully initialized. Swauth is typically initialized using a command similar to the following one:

```
swauth-prep -A http://127.0.0.1:8080/auth/ -K swauthkey
```

Note that there is no output when this command is completed successfully. The value for `swauthkey` in the command should match the value in your `/etc/proxy-server.conf` file under the `[filter:swauth]` section. The value for `super_admin_key` should be listed here.

If you run into unauthorized errors, similar to what we saw in the TempAuth section, you will want to confirm that your accounts and users have been set up in Swauth. You can do this by leveraging the `swauth-list` command:

```
swauth-list -A http://127.0.0.1:8080/auth/ -K swauthkey
```

Again, the value passed into the `-K` argument should match the entry of `super_admin_key` in the `[Filter:swauth]` section of the `proxy-server.conf` file. Upon successful execution, this command will return an output similar to this:

```
root@ost-swift:~# swauth-list -A http://127.0.0.1:8080/auth/ -K swauthkey
{"accounts": [{"name": "test"}]}
```

This command returns a list of the accounts (projects/tenants) loaded into Swauth. Likewise, you can list the users under an account using the following command:

```
swauth-list -A http://127.0.0.1:8080/auth/ -K swauthkey test
```

This command looks very similar to the command used earlier to list accounts. The only difference is that we will include the name of the account we want to list users for. In this example, the name of the account is test, and it is the last argument sent to the preceding command. The output of this command is as follows:

```
{services: {storage: {default: local, local: http://127.0.0.1:8080/v1/AUTH
_1d3f5917-2156-452a-8184-4f63378c94a5}}, account_id: AUTH_1d3f5917-2156-45
2a-8184-4f63378c94a5, users: [{name: tester}]}
```

In this output, you will see a section titled users, which provides a list of users on the test account. The output displays one user under the test account with a username tester. If, for some reason, these commands do not return the accounts or users you are expecting, then you can add users using a command similar to the following one:

```
swauth-add-user -A http://104.239.130.27:8080/auth/ -K swauthkey -a test
tester testing
```

There are additional swauth commands that may prove useful when troubleshooting. These commands are given in the following list:

- swauth-add-account
- swauth-add-user
- swauth-cleanup-tokens
- swauth-delete-account
- swauth-delete-user
- swauth-list
- swauth-prep
- swauth-set-account-service

Using the preceding commands, you can troubleshoot and correct most errors with your Swauth data.

Swift with Keystone

Most deployments of Swift will most likely be configured to use Keystone, the OpenStack Identity service, for authentication. When troubleshooting a Swift deployment using Keystone, it is wise to start by making sure that Keystone is operating appropriately. Be sure to review *Chapter 2, Troubleshooting OpenStack Identity*, for tips on troubleshooting that service.

Swift users

Most installations will include a Swift service user that the object storage service will use to interact with Keystone. Make sure that the Swift user exists, and the password for this user has been set accurately in Keystone and in the `proxy-server.conf` file. You can use the OpenStack client to check whether the Swift user exists:

```
openstack user list
```

When you run the preceding `user list` command, as demonstrated, you will see a list of users recorded in Keystone. Make sure that there is a Swift user present.

```
[root@ost-swift:~# openstack user list
+--------------------------------------+--------+
| ID                                   | Name   |
+--------------------------------------+--------+
| 439a34fc60da4bceb188d8dfb811240c     | nova   |
| 4f98c8914e7542429ae39270151e747e     | swift  |
| 5380291587c640eeaf27ee29b7fa5360     | ec2    |
| 9f7b728282344cf09970755c13d1e0aa     | admin  |
| b76cb0e96f7b4ccfa66bccd50bcec675     | glance |
+--------------------------------------+--------+
```

If the Swift user has not been created already, you can create this user using the Keystone client:

```
keystone user-create --name swift --pass swiftpass --tenant service
```

Likewise, you can create the Swift user using the OpenStack client:

```
openstack user create swift --password swiftpass --project service
```

Whether you are using the Keystone client or the OpenStack client, be sure to set a secure password. Once the Swift user has been created, this user will need to be assigned the admin role under the service project/tenant.

Once the Swift user has been created, check whether you have configured the Swift proxy server with the correct credentials. Confirm the credentials at `/etc/swift/proxy-server.conf` under the `[filter:authtoken]` section. Take the following screenshot, for example:

```
1    [filter:authtoken]
2    paste.filter_factory = keystonemiddleware.auth_token:filter_factory
3    auth_uri = http://127.0.0.1:5000
4    auth_url = http://127.0.0.1:35357
5    auth_plugin = password
6    project_domain_id = default
7    user_domain_id = default
8    project_name = service
9    username = swift
10   password = swiftpass
11   delay_auth_decision = true
```

Summary

Swift is an object storage service that is designed to expect failure and boasts built-in resiliency. There are some scenarios where Swift will require troubleshooting. As we have seen, Swift offers several authentication options and relies on several key processes. Learning to keep these elements running correctly will take you a long way in your efforts to troubleshoot Swift. In the next chapter, we will take a look at Heat, the OpenStack Orchestration service.

8

Troubleshooting the OpenStack the Orchestration Service

Heat is the code name for the OpenStack orchestration service. Much like a conductor works with a collection of musicians and leads them to make beautiful music together, so does Heat work with a collection of OpenStack services in an effort to make cloud building easier. Heat provides a means by which users can coordinate services such as Nova, Neutron, Glance, Keystone, and others. Heat makes it easy to plug the OpenStack services together into `Stack`. When it comes to troubleshooting Heat, there are two stages you will need to be concerned with. The first is Heat itself and the second is all the OpenStack services Heat leverages to do its job. In this chapter, we will look at the following topics:

- Troubleshooting Heat services
- Fixing Heat authentication issues
- Correcting common Heat template errors

Heat services

A properly running Heat installation will have at least two processes: the Heat API process (`heat-api`) and the Heat engine (`heat-engine`). In addition, you can also optionally run the Heat Cloud Formation compatibility API (`heat-api-cfn`). This API makes `heat` compatible with the API provided by the AWS Cloud Formation product. You can confirm that these processes are running by executing the following command:

```
ps -aux | grep heat
```

This command should return an output similar to the following output:

```
[root@ost-controller:~# ps -aux | grep heat
root      11153  0.0  0.0  11980    916 pts/6   S+   08:01   0:00 grep heat
heat      27367  0.0  1.4 181064 57184 ?        Ss   Feb20   0:00 /usr/bin/
python /usr/local/bin/heat-api --config-file=/etc/heat/heat.conf
heat      27420  0.0  1.4 179616 55552 ?        Ss   Feb20   0:00 /usr/bin/
python /usr/local/bin/heat-api-cfn --config-file=/etc/heat/heat.conf
heat      27423  0.0  1.4 181064 54488 ?        S    Feb20   0:00 /usr/bin/
python /usr/local/bin/heat-api --config-file=/etc/heat/heat.conf
heat      27424  0.0  1.4 181064 54492 ?        S    Feb20   0:00 /usr/bin/
python /usr/local/bin/heat-api --config-file=/etc/heat/heat.conf
heat      27458  0.5  1.7 189712 65724 ?        Ss   Feb20   3:11 /usr/bin/
python /usr/local/bin/heat-engine --config-file=/etc/heat/heat.conf
heat      27496  0.0  1.8 277496 69428 ?        S    Feb20   0:05 /usr/bin/
python /usr/local/bin/heat-engine --config-file=/etc/heat/heat.conf
heat      27497  0.0  1.8 277760 69460 ?        S    Feb20   0:05 /usr/bin/
python /usr/local/bin/heat-engine --config-file=/etc/heat/heat.conf
heat      27498  0.0  1.7 277500 69228 ?        S    Feb20   0:05 /usr/bin/
python /usr/local/bin/heat-engine --config-file=/etc/heat/heat.conf
heat      27499  0.0  1.8 277632 69468 ?        S    Feb20   0:05 /usr/bin/
python /usr/local/bin/heat-engine --config-file=/etc/heat/heat.conf
```

You can also leverage the `pgrep` command to check the Heat processes:

```
pgrep -l heat
```

The output from this command will be similar to the following output:

```
[root@ost-controller:~# pgrep -l heat
27367 heat-api
27420 heat-api-cfn
27423 heat-api
27424 heat-api
27458 heat-engine
27496 heat-engine
27497 heat-engine
27498 heat-engine
27499 heat-engine
```

Running heat-api

One way to confirm that the `heat-api` process is running as expected is to use the Heat command-line tool. For example, you can execute the `stack-list` command to check this:

```
heat stack-list
```

When the `heat-api` process runs as expected, this command returns a list of your current stacks or an empty list if you haven't created any stacks yet, as demonstrated in the following screenshot:

```
[root@ost-controller:~# heat stack-list
+----+------------+--------------+---------------+--------------+
| id | stack_name | stack_status | creation_time | updated_time |
+----+------------+--------------+---------------+--------------+
+----+------------+--------------+---------------+--------------+
```

Suppose that you attempt to use the Heat command-line tool and you receive an error as follows:

```
Unable to establish connection to http://127.0.0.1:8004/v1/01c77a30b0e442c
9afa73117a407a277/stacks?
```

This error message is a clear sign that your `heat-api` process is not running. You can also leverage the `--debug` argument on the `heat` command in order to see more detail of the error:

```
heat --debug stack-list
```

As with most of the other OpenStack command-line clients, the `--debug` argument is available as a tool to assist you in troubleshooting.

You can also use the Heat API to confirm the successful status of the `heat-api` process. If you run a basic query on the Heat API, it should return a list of the API versions supported by Heat. Take the following line of code as an example:

```
curl -i -H "Content-Type: application/json" http://127.0.0.1:8004/
```

The value returned from the preceding `curl` call should be similar to the following output:

```
[root@ost-controller:~# curl -i -H "Content-Type: application/json" http://
127.0.0.1:8004/
HTTP/1.1 300 Multiple Choices
Content-Type: application/json; charset=UTF-8
Content-Length: 116
X-Openstack-Request-Id: req-ca9c5251-1939-4839-90c5-2cb34ad9f0dd
Date: Mon, 22 Feb 2016 02:15:17 GMT

{"versions": [{"status": "CURRENT", "id": "v1.0", "links": [{"href": "http
://127.0.0.1:8004/v1/", "rel": "self"}]}]}root@ost-controller:~#
```

When you run the preceding `curl` command and `heat-api` does not run, you will see an error similar to the one shown here:

```
[root@ost-controller:~# curl -i -H "Content-Type: application/json" http://
127.0.0.1:8004/
curl: (7) Failed to connect to 127.0.0.1 port 8004: Connection refused
```

To start `heat-api`, you can typically use one of the following commands:

```
start heat-api
```

```
service heat-api start
```

Once you have attempted to start the service, use the `ps` or `pgrep` commands, as demonstrated earlier, to confirm that the service has started successfully. If the service does not appear to start as expected, you should attempt to start it manually. When starting the service manually, any error that occurs during the startup process will be printed directly to the console for further troubleshooting. To start `heat-api` manually, you will have to run the following command:

```
sudo -u heat heat-api --config-file=/etc/heat/heat.conf
```

Once you execute the preceding command, you should see startup log messages printed to the console. Check for any errors, failures, or trace messages. You may also want to execute `heat` commands to test whether `heat-api` is working, for example, the `heat stack-list` command we used earlier. If the `heat-api` service works as expected when you start it manually, but incorrectly when started with `start heat-api` or `service heat-api start`, then you will want to validate the `init` scripts for the `heat` service. Check your `init` script for the correct path to the configuration files and log file. Also, make sure that your Linux `heat` user has write permissions for the `config` directory and logging file, for example, `/etc/init/heat-api.conf`.

Running heat-engine

Similar to our approach of troubleshooting the `heat-api` process, we can confirm whether or not the `heat-engine` service is running as expected by executing a `heat` command:

```
heat stack-list
```

As we saw in the preceding `heat-api` section, this command should return a list of stacks or an empty list if your installation does not have any stacks. If the command times out with an error similar to the following one, this is a sign that there may be trouble with the `heat-engine` process:

```
root@ost-controller:~# heat stack-list
ERROR: Timed out waiting for a reply to message ID 91e953c2a0854f6f87bcfd3
ab2f36dbe
```

You can further troubleshoot this type of error by looking at the heat logs. For example, the following trace is printed to /var/log/heat/heat.log in my installation. You can find these logs on the server running the heat-api process. In most deployments, this will be the controller node. The logging directory is set in the heat.conf file at /etc/heat/heat.conf under the attribute named log_dir.

```
2016-02-21 20:19:33.626 22970 ERROR heat.common.wsgi [req-5f063c43-9fef-4
26c-951c-82ce3424a96d - demo - - -] Unexpected error occurred serving API
: Timed out waiting for a reply to message ID 91e953c2a0854f6f87bcfd3ab2f
36dbe
```

The Heat command-line tool offers the service-list command, which can be useful when troubleshooting the heat-engine process. When heat-engine runs as expected, the output will be similar to the output shown here:

```
root@ost-controller:~# heat service-list
+----------------+-------------+------------------------------------------+
----------+---------+---------------------------------------+---------+
| hostname       | binary      | engine_id                                |
host         | topic   | updated_at                  | status  |
+----------------+-------------+------------------------------------------+
----------+---------+---------------------------------------+---------+
| ost-controller | heat-engine | 00c07a68-bce8-4b89-8854-9eea5abe5ae4    |
127.0.0.1    | engine  | 2016-02-22T15:54:25.000000  | up      |
| ost-controller | heat-engine | 18da6616-22b3-4307-b85d-20e3a9defed4    |
127.0.0.1    | engine  | 2016-02-22T15:54:25.000000  | up      |
| ost-controller | heat-engine | 4fcff217-651f-4d6f-9f85-e2285b1642eb    |
127.0.0.1    | engine  | 2016-02-22T15:54:25.000000  | up      |
| ost-controller | heat-engine | fd547120-07db-4a89-9f78-73c49872fa96    |
127.0.0.1    | engine  | 2016-02-22T15:54:25.000000  | up      |
+----------------+-------------+------------------------------------------+
----------+---------+---------------------------------------+---------+
```

The heat service-list command will return a list of those Heat engines that are active in your installation. If you do not have any active Heat engines, the output returned will be similar to the output shown in this screenshot:

```
root@ost-controller:~# heat service-list
ERROR: All heat engines are down.
```

Each of the methods in this section will help you diagnose a problem with the `heat-engine` process. If you determine that the process is not running, it can be started with one of the following commands:

```
start heat-engine
```

```
service heat-engine start
```

Once you have started the `heat-engine` process, you can confirm that it is running successfully using the `ps` or `pgrep` command, as demonstrated earlier. If the process does not start as expected, you can attempt to run the process manually. When you start the process manually, the startup output will be printed to the terminal and may prove useful for further troubleshooting. To start the `heat` manually, you will need to run the following command:

```
sudo -u heat heat-engine --config-file=/etc/heat/heat.conf
```

Check the output of the preceding command for any ERRORS, WARNINGS, or failure lines. If `heat-engine` starts successfully when it's run manually, but does not start as expected when you use the start or service commands, you will want to check the `heat-engine init` scripts. Check your `init` script for the correct path to the configuration files and log file. Also make sure that your Linux `heat` user has write permissions for the `config` directory and logging file.

Heat authentication

Like each of the other OpenStack services that we have seen up until this point, Heat also leverages Keystone to manage its authentication. Therefore, the successful operation of Heat depends on a working and properly configured Keystone installation.

The Keystone service

If there is a problem with Keystone, it will not take long for you to notice this. If you attempt to run the `stack-list` command when Keystone is not working, you will see an error similar to the following one:

```
Unable to establish connection to http://127.0.0.1:35357/v2.0/tokens
```

Note that, in the error message, the connection URL is for the Keystone service. This is a clear sign that something is wrong with the Keystone endpoint or process. In this situation, you want to make sure that Keystone is up and running correctly. If you need to troubleshoot Keystone, refer to *Chapter 2, Troubleshooting OpenStack Identity*.

Auth credentials

One issue that can be difficult to troubleshoot is incorrect credentials. When you attempt to run `heat` commands with incorrect credentials, you will see an error similar to the following one:

```
root@ost-controller:~# heat stack-list
ERROR: 503 Service Unavailable

The server is currently unavailable. Please try again at a later time.
```

The server unavailable error may lead you to believe that the `heat-api` or `heat-engine` service is unavailable. If you run the command with the `--debug` argument, you will find more information that is useful when troubleshooting:

heat --debug stack-list

The output of the preceding command will look like what is shown in the following screenshot. When using the `--debug` switch with the `heat` command-line tool, debug information will be printed to the console along with the output of the command. This debug information can provide more clues to assist in your troubleshooting. As demonstrated here, you will be able to see information from the API calls made by the `heat` command-line tool:

```
INFO (connectionpool) Starting new HTTP connection (1): 127.0.0.1
DEBUG (connectionpool) "GET /v1/ec03b1241e884a8b93ede7d73563617c/stacks HT
TP/1.1" 503 100
DEBUG (session) RESP: [503] Date: Mon, 22 Feb 2016 03:31:03 GMT Connection
: keep-alive Content-Type: text/plain; charset=UTF-8 Content-Length: 100 X
-Openstack-Request-Id: req-cdd402d5-533d-4811-8897-4ec42dde41c3
RESP BODY: 503 Service Unavailable

The server is currently unavailable. Please try again at a later time.
```

As we troubleshoot the preceding error, we can use the techniques discussed earlier in this chapter to make sure that the `heat-api` and `heat-engine` services are working as expected. In addition to this, because we know that Heat relies upon many of the other OpenStack services, we should confirm the successful operation of Keystone, Glance, Nova, Neutron, and any other services we may be leveraging in our Heat templates. After you have confirmed the services, you should double-check your Heat configuration.

The `503 Service Unavailable` error usually points to the fact that the `heat` service user you are using is not configured correctly. To confirm the service user for Heat, take a look at the Heat configuration file, typically located at `/etc/heat/heat.conf`. In that file, under the `[keystone_authtoken]` stanza, there will be a username and password, as shown in the following screenshot:

```
1   [keystone_authtoken]
2   auth_uri = http://keystoneserver:5000
3   auth_url = http://keystoneserver:35357
4   auth_plugin = password
5   project_domain_id = default
6   user_domain_id = default
7   project_name = service
8   username = heat
9   password = heatpassword
```

Confirm that the username and password set in this configuration file are the same username and password that were set in Keystone. You can confirm this by attempting a Keystone auth token call with that username and password.

```
1   curl -i \
2       -H "Content-Type: application/json" \
3       -d '
4   {
5       "auth": {
6           "identity": {
7               "methods": [
8                   "password"
9               ],
10              "password": {
11                  "user": {
12                      "name": "heat",
13                      "domain": {
14                          "id": "default"
15                      },
16                      "password": "heatpassword"
17                  }
18              }
19          }
20      }
21  }' \
22      http://127.0.0.1:5000/v3/auth/tokens; echo
```

The preceding `curl` command demonstrates how we can use the Keystone API to authenticate the Heat user. In the preceding command, the username is on line **12** and is set to `heat`. The password for the `heat` user is set on line **16**. It is set to `heatpassword` in the example.

If the username and password are correct, this call will return successfully with an HTTP 201 response and provide an `authtoken` in the `X-Subject-Token` header.

```
HTTP/1.1 201 Created
Date: Mon, 22 Feb 2016 03:37:42 GMT
Server: Apache/2.4.7 (Ubuntu)
X-Subject-Token: 4f9be876c5a24aec9e335bbb57526415
Vary: X-Auth-Token
x-openstack-request-id: req-cbbe1156-d479-4d69-a5dd-c1922b70e339
Content-Length: 296
Content-Type: application/json

{"token": {"methods": ["password"], "expires_at": "2016-02-22T04:37:42.689
453Z", "extras": {}, "user": {"domain": {"id": "default", "name": "Default
"}, "id": "c7f777b4841741b29941abcb1ef77c16", "name": "heat"}, "audit_ids"
: ["m_LVXnOIRW6FGpIbzjctLA"], "issued_at": "2016-02-22T03:37:42.689508Z"}}
```

If the password is incorrect, the output from this `curl` call will be similar to the following output:

```
HTTP/1.1 401 Unauthorized
Date: Mon, 22 Feb 2016 03:36:19 GMT
Server: Apache/2.4.7 (Ubuntu)
Vary: X-Auth-Token
x-openstack-request-id: req-75eddf3c-bdcd-4b0d-82e7-356afe02b274
WWW-Authenticate: Keystone uri="http://localhost:5000"
Content-Length: 140
Content-Type: application/json

{"error": {"message": "Invalid username or password (Disable debug mode to
 suppress these details.)", "code": 401, "title": "Unauthorized"}}
```

This `401 Unauthorized` error is a great clue, indicating that there is a problem with the username and password you are using. To resolve this issue, you either need to change the username and password in the `/etc/heat/heat.conf` under the `[keystone_authtoken]` stanza or you can update the password in Keystone to match what you have configured in the Heat configuration file. To update the password for the heat user, you can use a command similar to the one given here:

```
openstack user set --password <newpassword> heat
```

This command will update the password for the heat user, but it does not return any output upon successful completion. You can confirm that the password has been successfully updated by running the `curl` command that we discussed in the previous section.

Heat template errors

Once you have confirmed that the `heat-api` and `heat-engine` processes are running as expected, and your authentication credentials are correct in Keystone and the `heat.conf` file, you should be able to start creating stacks. The details on how to create a Heat stack are beyond the scope of this book; however, once you have created a stack, you can check its progress by running the `heat stack-list` command. The output of the column titled `stack_status` will indicate whether or not the stack has been successfully launched. If, for some reason, your stack does not get completed successfully, `stack_status` will be equal to `CREATE_FAILED`, as demonstrated in the following screenshot:

```
root@ost-controller:~# heat stack-list
+-----------------------------------+------------+--------------+------
----------------+-----------------+
| id                                | stack_name | stack_status | crea
tion_time      | updated_time   |
+-----------------------------------+------------+--------------+------
----------------+-----------------+
| 9e447891-4b6b-45ec-a644-d1a67cc6b22f | teststack  | CREATE_FAILED | 2016
-02-22T14:43:33 | None           |
+-----------------------------------+------------+--------------+------
----------------+-----------------+
```

If you have a failed stack, you can begin to troubleshoot the failure using the `event-list` command of `heat`. This command will output the steps `heat` has followed to create the stack and any errors `heat` encountered in the process.

```
root@ost-controller:~# heat event-list teststack
+--------------+-----------------------------------+--------------------+
---------------
| resource_name | id                               | resource_status_r
eason
               | resource_status  | event_time         |
+--------------+-----------------------------------+--------------------+
---------------
| teststack    | 8dd55cc5-82e1-4289-b433-cd34df21d368 | Stack CREATE star
ted
               | CREATE_IN_PROGRESS | 2016-02-22T14:43:33 |
| my_instance  | c1fbab4a-7325-47fb-95b2-9ef646b800d4 | state changed
               | CREATE_IN_PROGRESS | 2016-02-22T14:43:33 |
| my_instance  | aeaae3f9-1dee-486d-8a94-9d732e63bcff | ResourceInError:
resources.my_instance: Went to status ERROR due to "Message: No valid host
was found. There are not enough hosts available., Code: 500"
               | CREATE_FAILED    | 2016-02-22T14:46:26 |
| my_instance  | 71afe58c-330b-426b-a806-348c6cd9dd5e | state changed
```

Summary

The OpenStack Orchestration service provides a simple means to control the life cycle of your OpenStack infrastructure. Heat relies deeply on the other OpenStack services in order to provide its functionality. When troubleshooting Heat, it's important to make sure that the `heat-api` and `heat-engine` processes are running. Make sure that Keystone is correctly configured with the appropriate username and password. You will also want to make sure Keystone is up and running. Finally, if you run into trouble with a particular stack, remember to use `heat event-list` to help troubleshoot the issue. In the next chapter, we will begin to look at Ceilometer, the OpenStack telemetry service.

9
Troubleshooting the OpenStack Telemetry Service

Ceilometer is the code name of the OpenStack telemetry service. Ceilometer is responsible for metering in an OpenStack cluster. This service captures data about events, notifications, and measurements throughout the cluster. This data can be used for multiple purposes, including billing, monitoring, and autoscaling. Ceilometer works in conjunction with other OpenStack services in order to provide its functionality. In this chapter, we will explore the following topics:

- Troubleshooting Ceilometer processes
- Resolving Ceilometer authentication issues
- Troubleshooting issues between Ceilometer, the message broker, and the database
- Fixing issues with Ceilometer meters for Glance and Nova

Ceilometer processes

A working Ceilometer installation will have several processes running, some of which are as follows:

- `ceilometer-api`
- `ceilometer-collector`
- `ceilometer-polling`
- `ceilometer-agent-notification`

When troubleshooting Ceilometer, an effective place to start is ensuring that each of the preceding processes run. As we've seen before, we can verify this by running either ps -aux or pgrep on Ceilometer. Take the following command, for example:

```
[root@ost-controller:~# ps -aux | grep ceilometer
ceilome+ 11411  0.0  1.4 175296 55780 ?          Ss   09:27   0:01 /usr/bin/
python /usr/local/bin/ceilometer-api --log-dir=/var/log/ceilometer
ceilome+ 11528  0.0  1.0 130668 40388 ?          Ss   09:27   0:01 /usr/bin/
python /usr/local/bin/ceilometer-collector --log-dir=/var/log/ceilometer
ceilome+ 11568  0.1  1.3 210132 53412 ?          Ss   09:27   0:03 /usr/bin/
python /usr/local/bin/ceilometer-polling --log-dir=/var/log/ceilometer
ceilome+ 11721  0.8  1.2 134828 48844 ?          Ss   09:27   0:19 /usr/bin/
python /usr/local/bin/ceilometer-agent-notification --log-dir=/var/log/cei
lometer
root     17157  0.0  0.0  11984   924 pts/10    S+   10:05   0:00 grep ceil
ometer
```

Alternatively, you can use the pgrep command to retrieve similar information. An example is included in the following screenshot:

```
[root@ost-controller:~# pgrep -l ceilometer
11411 ceilometer-api
11528 ceilometer-coll
11568 ceilometer-poll
11721 ceilometer-agen
```

If any of these processes are not running as expected, you can search the log files for possible clues. The log files for Ceilometer are typically stored at /var/log/ceilometer, but you can confirm the log file location by checking the Ceilometer configuration file for the value of the log_dir variable. If the log files are empty or do not provide any clues, you can attempt to start the services manually, which will cause the output to be printed to the console as the process starts up. For example, to start ceilometer-api manually, you would use a command similar to the following:

```
sudo -u ceilometer ceilometer-api --config-file=/etc/ceilometer/
ceilometer.conf --log-file=/var/log/ceilometer/ceilometer-api.log
```

If there are errors during startup, examine the output carefully for clues pointing to the root cause.

Ceilometer authentication

Like most of the other OpenStack services that we've seen up until this point, Ceilometer relies on Keystone for authentication. Therefore, you want to pay attention to the Ceilometer logs as well as the Keystone logs. If you encounter auth problems with Ceilometer, start by taking a look at the ceilometer-api.log file.

It will be helpful to use grep on this log file, to search for ERROR or WARNING indicators. You may also want to use grep for 404 or 401 responses. If you find authentication errors in the API log, you will most likely find corresponding log lines in the Keystone log file.

When troubleshooting authentication errors, make sure that the authentication credentials in the [keystone_authtoken] stanza of the ceilometer.conf file match the actual values loaded into Keystone for the Ceilometer user. You can test your Ceilometer credentials using the Keystone API.

Ceilometer dependencies

Ceilometer has a few external dependencies that troubleshooters need to be familiar with. Like the other OpenStack services, Ceilometer makes heavy use of the message broker. In most installations, the message broker will be RabbitMQ. Ceilometer will read events and notifications from the message queue, and translate that data into meters. In addition, Ceilometer relies on a database to store all the meters, events, notifications, and so on. The recommended database for Ceilometer is MongoDB. Ceilometer introduces the MongoDB noSQL database, while most other OpenStack projects use a relational database, such as MySQL. When troubleshooting Ceilometer, you want to make sure that each of these dependencies are in good working order.

The message broker

During the Ceilometer installation process, you will need to make sure that RabbitMQ, or another message broker, is installed and configured properly. The configuration for the message broker can be found in Ceilometer's primary configuration file, ceilometer.conf. In this file, you should confirm all the values under the [oslo_messaging_rabbit] stanza or the [oslo_messaging_qpid] stanza if you are using qpid in place of RabbitMQ. Finally, you should confirm the values under the [oslo_messaging_amqp] section.

After you have confirmed the configuration for the message broker, you want to make sure that the broker is up and running. We can start by checking the process as shown here:

```
root@ost-controller:~# ps -aux | grep rabbitmq-server
root      20353  0.0  0.0  11980   920 pts/10   S+   10:09   0:00 grep rabb
itmq-server
rabbitmq  31611  0.0  0.0   4440   652 ?        S    09:46   0:00 /bin/sh /
usr/sbin/rabbitmq-server
```

Again, we can leverage the `pgrep` command to achieve a similar effect, as shown in the following screenshot:

```
root@ost-controller:~# pgrep -l rabbit
31611 rabbitmq-server
```

If you are using RabbitMQ, you can leverage the `rabbitmqctl` tool when troubleshooting. For example, to check the status of RabbitMQ, you can run this code:

```
root@ost-controller:~# rabbitmqctl status
Status of node 'rabbit@ost-controller' ...
[{pid,31620},
 {running_applications,[{rabbit,"RabbitMQ","3.2.4"},
                        {os_mon,"CPO  CXC 138 46","2.2.14"},
                        {mnesia,"MNESIA  CXC 138 12","4.11"},
                        {xmerl,"XML parser","1.3.5"},
                        {sasl,"SASL  CXC 138 11","2.3.4"},
                        {stdlib,"ERTS  CXC 138 10","1.19.4"},
                        {kernel,"ERTS  CXC 138 10","2.16.4"}]},
 {os,{unix,linux}},
 {erlang_version,"Erlang R16B03 (erts-5.10.4) [source] [64-bit] [smp:2:2]
[async-threads:30] [kernel-poll:true]\n"},
 {memory,[{total,65272560},
          {connection_procs,513368},
          {queue_procs,286984},
          {plugins,0},
          {other_proc,13425704},
          {mnesia,112992},
          {mgmt_db,0},
          {msg_index,48016},
          {other_ets,791088},
          {binary,28909200},
          {code,16522377},
          {atom,594537},
          {other_system,4068294}]},
 {vm_memory_high_watermark,0.4},
 {vm_memory_limit,1577284403},
 {disk_free_limit,50000000},
 {disk_free,44245573632},
 {file_descriptors,[{total_limit,924},
                    {total_used,14},
                    {sockets_limit,829},
                    {sockets_used,12}]},
 {processes,[{limit,1048576},{used,265}]},
 {run_queue,0},
 {uptime,1731}]
...done.
```

The preceding screenshot is a truncated example of the output returned from the `rabbitmqctl status` command. If you attempt to run this command and receive an output as shown in the following screenshot, this indicates that RabbitMQ is not running:

```
[root@ost-controller:~# rabbitmqctl status
Status of node 'rabbit@ost-controller' ...
Error: unable to connect to node 'rabbit@ost-controller': nodedown

DIAGNOSTICS
===========

nodes in question: ['rabbit@ost-controller']

hosts, their running nodes and ports:
- ost-controller: [{rabbitmqctl27273,41908}]

current node details:
- node name: 'rabbitmqctl27273@ost-controller'
- home dir: /var/lib/rabbitmq
- cookie hash: hY/q1bh20AJifSDTJWP91A==
```

Start the service by running a command similar to this:

```
service rabbitmq-server start
```

You can also use the `rabbitmqctl` tool to view the various queues and messages used by Ceilometer. In the following screenshot, we execute the `list_queues` command, which returns a list of message queues along with the number of messages waiting in each queue:

```
[root@ost-controller:~# rabbitmqctl list_queues
Listing queues ...
engine  0
engine.127.0.0.1        0
engine_fanout_08503ee500f1453e9632c7d27c35ad3a  0
engine_fanout_434b74024c39433bbdcc698623c80708  0
engine_fanout_7587ce5835eb448a85810c023eae944d  0
engine_fanout_8fea7bee619c414981cbdbe56903daf1  0
heat-engine-listener    0
heat-engine-listener.00c07a68-bce8-4b89-8854-9eea5abe5ae4       0
heat-engine-listener.18da6616-22b3-4307-b85d-20e3a9defed4       0
heat-engine-listener.4fcff217-651f-4d6f-9f85-e2285b1642eb       0
heat-engine-listener.fd547120-07db-4a89-9f78-73c49872fa96       0
heat-engine-listener_fanout_1afc593350434fe88826e02e3294a1e6    0
heat-engine-listener_fanout_23e89c8157a944da88b8ff34d0f5550c    0
heat-engine-listener_fanout_78fd9a89443a4843b216ff7a4ada5a7c    0
heat-engine-listener_fanout_c4b8ab6d0203463bb21e6084c14d2fa0    0
reply_fec2654e86c7455ea227c2d4f544b50a  0
...done.
```

The preceding output is edited to highlight the metering and notification queues leveraged by Ceilometer. This command is useful to monitor the messages consumed by Ceilometer.

Databases

As mentioned earlier, most Ceilometer installations leverage MongoDB as the database. You can confirm that MongoDB is running by executing the `pgrep` or `ps --aux` commands, as demonstrated in the following lines of code:

```
[root@ost-controller:~# pgrep -l mongo
10449 mongod
```

Using the `ps -aux` command, we can look at additional information about the running `mongo` processes, as shown in the next output:

```
[root@ost-controller:~# ps -aux | grep mongo
root      9150  0.0  0.0  11980   916 pts/10   S+   10:34   0:00 grep mong
o
mongodb  10449  0.2  1.0 551028 41096 ?        Ssl  09:26   0:09 /usr/bin/
mongod --config /etc/mongodb.conf
```

MongoDB provides a command-line utility that can be leveraged for management, but it is also useful for troubleshooting. You can confirm that this utility is up and running by typing `mongo` into the terminal, as shown in the following screenshot:

```
[root@ost-controller:~# mongo
MongoDB shell version: 2.4.9
connecting to: test
Welcome to the MongoDB shell.
For interactive help, type "help".
For more comprehensive documentation, see
        http://docs.mongodb.org/
Questions? Try the support group
        http://groups.google.com/group/mongodb-user
> []
```

You can confirm that the Ceilometer database has been created successfully by asking `mongo` to show the current databases:

```
> show databases
admin    (empty)
ceilometer       0.203125GB
local    0.078125GB
> []
```

You can switch to the Ceilometer database in order to query it further by executing the `use` command, as shown in the following screenshot:

```
> use ceilometer
switched to db ceilometer
>
```

From this point, you can find all the collections (tables) under the Ceilometer database by running the `show collections` command:

```
> show collections
alarm
alarm_history
event
meter
resource
system.indexes
system.users
>
```

From here, you can query all the documents in a given collection by utilizing the `db.collection.find()` method. For example, the following command will query all the documents in the `meter` collection:

```
> db.meter.find()
{ "_id" : ObjectId("56cb4d51176d3701905b048d"), "counter_name" : "image",
"user_id" : null, "resource_id" : "2a61e863-3122-4596-b8cd-1885cb2db074",
"timestamp" : ISODate("2016-02-22T18:02:51.958Z"), "message_signature" : "
", "message_id" : "7d8d195a-d98e-11e5-9a9c-bc764e207ebd", "source" : "open
stack", "counter_unit" : "image", "counter_volume" : 1, "recorded_at" : IS
ODate("2016-02-22T18:02:57.536Z"), "project_id" : "da76e9a471d8411a875b767
db29f2b24", "resource_metadata" : { "status" : "active", "name" : "cirros-
qcow2", "deleted" : false, "container_format" : "bare", "created_at" : "20
16-02-22T17:21:09.000000", "disk_format" : "qcow2", "updated_at" : "2016-0
2-22T17:21:09.000000", "properties" : { }, "protected" : false, "checksum
" : "ee1eca47dc88f4879d8a229cc70a07c6", "min_disk" : 0, "is_public" : true
, "deleted_at" : null, "min_ram" : 0, "size" : 13287936 }, "counter_type"
: "gauge" }
```

The preceding output is truncated, but it gives you an idea of the type of data returned by the query. When troubleshooting, if your API calls or command-line client queries do not return meter data, you can check the database to confirm whether or not this data is being persisted properly.

You can narrow down your queries if you are looking for specific documents or fields by leveraging Mongo's query and projection operators. For example, to list all the counter_name values in the meter collection, you can run this code:

```
> db.meter.find({},{counter_name: 1})
{ "_id" : ObjectId("56cb4d51176d3701905b048d"), "counter_name" : "image" }
{ "_id" : ObjectId("56cb4d51176d3701905b048e"), "counter_name" : "image.si
ze" }
{ "_id" : ObjectId("56cb4d51176d3701905b048f"), "counter_name" : "image" }
{ "_id" : ObjectId("56cb4d51176d3701905b0490"), "counter_name" : "image.si
ze" }
{ "_id" : ObjectId("56cb4f82176d37254dda3087"), "counter_name" : "image.si
ze" }
{ "_id" : ObjectId("56cb4f82176d37254dda3088"), "counter_name" : "image.si
ze" }
{ "_id" : ObjectId("56cb4f82176d37254dda3089"), "counter_name" : "image" }
{ "_id" : ObjectId("56cb4f82176d37254dda308a"), "counter_name" : "image" }
{ "_id" : ObjectId("56cb5007176d3730488cde68"), "counter_name" : "image" }
{ "_id" : ObjectId("56cb5007176d3730488cde69"), "counter_name" : "image.si
ze" }
```

The command-line client

The Ceilometer command-line client tool is critical when troubleshooting this service. It is often the quickest way to test and identify issues within the service. Typing ceilometer help in the terminal will give you a list of the available commands. While covering all the Ceilometer commands is beyond the scope of this book, the commands that follow will aid your troubleshooting process.

The meter list command

The meter list command will allow you to see each of the meters tracked by Ceilometer. This command is also a good way to confirm that Ceilometer is working as expected. Errors or empty values returned from this command are clues to issues with the service or its configuration. When Ceilometer is working as expected, the meter-list command will return one or more meters, as shown in the following screenshot:

```
[root@ost-controller:~# ceilometer meter-list
+------------+--------+--------+------------------------------------------+------
----+----------------------------------+
| Name       | Type   | Unit   | Resource ID                              | User
ID  | Project ID                       |
+------------+--------+--------+------------------------------------------+------
----+----------------------------------+
| image      | gauge  | image  | 219f4c96-c03a-499e-b3de-3773ebb78392     | None
    | 2ecae889bd054f8faee11c4b7f0218e9 |
| image      | gauge  | image  | 2a61e863-3122-4596-b8cd-1885cb2db074     | None
    | da76e9a471d8411a875b767db29f2b24 |
| image.size | gauge  | B      | 219f4c96-c03a-499e-b3de-3773ebb78392     | None
    | 2ecae889bd054f8faee11c4b7f0218e9 |
| image.size | gauge  | B      | 2a61e863-3122-4596-b8cd-1885cb2db074     | None
    | da76e9a471d8411a875b767db29f2b24 |
+------------+--------+--------+------------------------------------------+------
----+----------------------------------+
```

If your meter list is empty, there are several troubleshooting steps that you should take. I recommend that you start with Glance and confirm whether Ceilometer is receiving metering data for the image service or not.

Glance meters

Assuming that Glance is installed and working, you will need to modify the `glance-api.conf` and `glance-registry.conf` files, which are typically located in the `/etc/glance` directory. You need to set the `notification_driver` and `notifier_strategy` in each of these files:

notification_driver = messagingv2

Once these settings have been added to the `glance-api.conf` and `glance-registry.conf` files, you will need to restart the `glance-api` and `glance-registry` processes for the configuration changes to take effect. After you have updated this setting, execute the `meter-list` command again and you should see the image meters appear.

Nova meters

Similar to Glance, Nova needs a few configuration updates if you want the service to provide metering data for Ceilometer. In the `/etc/nova/nova.conf` and `/etc/nova/nova-compute.conf` files:

instance_usage_audit = True

instance_usage_audit_period = hour

notify_on_state_change = vm_and_task_state

notification_driver = messagingv2

After you have made these modifications to the configuration files, restart the Nova service so that the configuration changes take effect. Try running the Ceilometer `meter-list` command again, and you should see values from OpenStack `Compute`.

The sample list

Another useful Ceilometer command is the `sample-list` command. This command will list the collection data representing samples for each meter. The command can be useful to check each of your meters and to ensure that you are receiving the data samples that you expect.

```
root@ost-controller:~# ceilometer sample-list
+------------------------------------------+------------------------------------------
----+-------------+--------+-------------+--------+-------------
-+
| ID                                       | Resource ID
   | Name         | Type  | Volume      | Unit  | Timestamp
|
+------------------------------------------+------------------------------------------
----+-------------+--------+-------------+--------+-------------
-+
| 03cf7960-d9ba-11e5-b50b-bc764e207ebd     | 2a61e863-3122-4596-b8cd-1885cb2db
074 | image        | gauge | 1.0         | image | 2016-02-22T23:14:25.574000
|
| 03cf7c62-d9ba-11e5-b50b-bc764e207ebd     | 219f4c96-c03a-499e-b3de-3773ebb78
392 | image        | gauge | 1.0         | image | 2016-02-22T23:14:25.574000
|
| 03c99568-d9ba-11e5-b50b-bc764e207ebd     | 2a61e863-3122-4596-b8cd-1885cb2db
074 | image.size   | gauge | 13287936.0  | B     | 2016-02-22T23:14:25.535000
|
| 03c99874-d9ba-11e5-b50b-bc764e207ebd     | 219f4c96-c03a-499e-b3de-3773ebb78
392 | image.size   | gauge | 13287936.0  | B     | 2016-02-22T23:14:25.535000
|
| 9dee4bea-d9b8-11e5-b50b-bc764e207ebd     | 2a61e863-3122-4596-b8cd-1885cb2db
074 | image        | gauge | 1.0         | image | 2016-02-22T23:04:25.151000
|
| 9dee4ed8-d9b8-11e5-b50b-bc764e207ebd     | 219f4c96-c03a-499e-b3de-3773ebb78
392 | image        | gauge | 1.0         | image | 2016-02-22T23:04:25.151000
|
```

The `sample-list` command also allows you to do some basic filtering and querying by passing the `--meter` and `--query` commands, respectively. For example, to see a sample list for all the instance meters for a particular resource, you could run the following command:

```
[root@ost-controller:~# ceilometer sample-list --meter instance --query re
source=9fd5325c-ee3b-4b6d-919d-715e898d06e4
+-----------------------------------------------------+---------+--------+--------+-----
-----+---------------------------------+
| Resource ID                                         | Name    | Type   | Volume | Unit
    | Timestamp                       |
+-----------------------------------------------------+---------+--------+--------+-----
----+---------------------------------+
| 9fd5325c-ee3b-4b6d-919d-715e898d06e4 | instance | gauge | 1.0     | inst
ance | 2016-02-23T20:57:33.033000 |
| 9fd5325c-ee3b-4b6d-919d-715e898d06e4 | instance | gauge | 1.0     | inst
ance | 2016-02-23T20:47:33.544000 |
+-----------------------------------------------------+---------+--------+--------+-----
----+---------------------------------+
```

For more complex queries against the sample data, you can leverage the Ceilometer `query-sample` command.

Summary

The OpenStack telemetry service is similar to other services when it comes to troubleshooting. A wise course of action is to check the various Ceilometer processes that we discussed in the previous sections. You will also want to confirm the successful operation of your message bus, of which Ceilometer will make heavy use. One unique dependency introduced by Ceilometer is the MongoDB database. You can confirm successful configuration and operation of Mongo using the tips discussed in this chapter. It is also worth noting that each service that you want to use with Ceilometer will need to be configured to send its metering data to Ceilometer. Finally, the Ceilometer command-line tool comes with several useful commands that can be leveraged when troubleshooting OpenStack telemetry as well as most of the other OpenStack services. In the next chapter, we will explore some tips to avoid emergency troubleshooting by watching our cluster's performance availability and reliability.

10

OpenStack Performance, Availability, and Reliability

We have covered a lot of errors and problems that you need to troubleshoot in a typical OpenStack installation. In this final chapter, we want to cover some of the chronic issues that might be early signs of trouble. This chapter is more about prevention and aims to help you avoid emergency troubleshooting as much as possible.

We will be looking at the following topics in this chapter:

- Databases
- RabbitMQ
- Services
- Community resources

Databases

As we have seen throughout this book, many OpenStack services make heavy use of databases. Production deployments typically use MySQL or Postgres as a backend database server. As you have learned, a failing or misconfigured database will quickly lead to trouble in your OpenStack cluster. Database problems can also present more subtle concerns that may grow into huge problems if neglected.

Availability

The database server can become a single point of failure if your database server is not deployed in a highly available configuration. OpenStack does not require a high-availability installation of your database, and as a result, many installations may skip this step. However, production deployments of OpenStack should take care to ensure that their database can survive the failure of a single database server.

MySQL with Galera Cluster

For installations that use the MySQL database engine, there are several options that can be used to cluster your installation. One popular method is to leverage Galera Cluster (http://galeracluster.com/). Galera Cluster for MySQL leverages synchronous replication and provides a multi-master cluster, which offers high availability for your OpenStack databases.

Postgres

Installations that use the Postgres database engine have several options: high availability, load balancing, and replication. Options include block device replication with DRBD, log shipping, master-standby replication based on triggers, statement based replication, and asynchronous multi-master replication. For details, refer to the Postgres high-availability guide (http://www.postgresql.org/docs/current/static/high-availability.html).

Performance

Database performance is one of those metrics that can degrade over time. For those administrators who do not pay attention, small problems in this area can eventually become large problems. A wise administrator will regularly monitor the performance of their database constantly to be on a lookout for slow queries, high-database loads, and other indications of trouble.

MySQL

There are several options to monitor your MySQL server, some of which are commercial and many that are open source. Administrators should evaluate the options available and select a solution that fits their current set of tools and operating environment. There are several performance metrics you will want to monitor. Some of them are discussed in the following sections.

Show status

The MySQL SHOW STATUS statement can be executed from the mysql Command Prompt. The output of this statement is server status information with over 300 variables that are reported. To narrow down this information, you can leverage a LIKE clause on the variable_name command to display the sections you are interested in. Here is an abbreviated list of the output returned by SHOW STATUS:

```
mysql> SHOW STATUS;
+--------------------------------------------------+-------------+
| Variable_name                                    | Value       |
```

```
+-------------------------------------------+-------------+
| Aborted_clients                           | 29          |
| Aborted_connects                          | 27          |
| Binlog_cache_disk_use                     | 0           |
| Binlog_cache_use                          | 0           |
| Binlog_stmt_cache_disk_use                | 0           |
| Binlog_stmt_cache_use                     | 0           |
| Bytes_received                            | 614         |
| Bytes_sent                                | 33178       |
```

Mytop

Mytop is a command-line utility inspired by the Linux `top` command. Mytop retrieves data from the MySql `SHOW PROCESSLIST` and `SHOW STATUS` commands. Data from these commands is refreshed, processed, and displayed in the output of the Mytop command. The Mytop output includes a header, which contains summary data, followed by a thread section.

The Mytop header section

Here is an example of the header output from the `Mytop` command:

```
MySQL on localhost (5.5.46)
load 1.01 0.85 0.79 4/538 23573 up 5+02:19:24 [14:35:24]
 Queries: 3.9M       qps:      9 Slow:        0.0         Se/In/Up/De(%):
49/00/08/00
 Sorts:       0 qps now:    10 Slow qps: 0.0  Threads:     30 (   1/    4)
40/00/12/00
 Cache Hits: 822.0 Hits/s:   0.0 Hits now:    0.0  Ratio:   0.0%
 Ratio now:   0.0%
 Key Efficiency: 97.3%  Bps in/out:  1.7k/ 3.1k   Now in/out:   1.0k/ 3.9k
```

As demonstrated in the preceding output, the header section for the `Mytop` command includes the following information:

- The hostname and MySQL version
- The server load
- The MySQL server uptime
- The total number of queries
- The average number of queries
- Slow queries
- The percentage of `Select`, `Insert`, `Update`, and `Delete` queries

- Queries per second
- Threads
- Cache hits
- Key efficiency

The Mytop thread section

The Mytop thread section will list as many threads as can be displayed. The threads are ordered by the Time column, which displays the threads idle time:

```
       Id      User        Host/IP           DB        Time    Cmd     State
Query
       --      ----        -------           --        ----    ---     -----
----------
      3461    neutron    174.143.201.98    neutron     5680    Sleep
      3477     glance    174.143.201.98     glance     1480    Sleep
      3491       nova    174.143.201.98       nova      880    Sleep
      3512       nova    174.143.201.98       nova      281    Sleep
      3487   keystone    174.143.201.98   keystone      280    Sleep
      3489     glance    174.143.201.98     glance      280    Sleep
      3511   keystone    174.143.201.98   keystone      280    Sleep
      3513    neutron    174.143.201.98    neutron      280    Sleep
      3505   keystone    174.143.201.98   keystone      279    Sleep
      3514   keystone    174.143.201.98   keystone      141    Sleep
      . . .
```

The Mytop thread section displays the ID of each thread followed by the user and host. Finally, this section will display the database, idle time, and state or command query. Mytop will allow you to keep an eye on the performance of your MySQL database server.

Percona Toolkit

Percona Toolkit is a very useful set of command-line tools that are used to perform MySQL operations and system tasks. The toolkit can be downloaded from Percona at https://www.percona.com/downloads/percona-toolkit/. The output from these tools can be fed into your monitoring system, allowing you to effectively monitor your MySQL installation.

Postgres

Like MySQL, the Postgres database also has a series of tools, which can be leveraged to monitor database performance. In addition to standard Linux troubleshooting tools, such as `top` and `ps`, Postgres also offers its own collection of statistics.

The PostgreSQL statistics collector

The statistics collector in Postgres allows you to collect data related to a server's activity. The statistics collected in this tool is varied, and may be helpful for troubleshooting or system monitoring. In order to leverage the statistics collector, you must turn on the functionality in the `postgresql.conf` file. The settings are commented out by default in the `RUNTIME STATISTICS` section of the configuration file. Uncomment the lines in the `Query/Index Statistics Collector` subsection:

```
#-------------------------------------------------------------------------
-------

# RUNTIME STATISTICS

#-------------------------------------------------------------------------
-------


# - Query/Index Statistics Collector -

track_activities = on
track_counts = on
track_io_timing = off
track_functions = none                   # none, pl, all
track_activity_query_size = 1024         # (change requires restart)
update_process_title = on
stats_temp_directory = 'pg_stat_tmp'
```

Once the statistics collector is configured, restart the database server or execute a `pg_ctl` command reload for the configuration to take effect. Once the collector has been configured, there will be a series of views created that are named with the prefix `pg_stat`. These views can be queried for relevant statistics in the Posgres database server.

Database backups

A diligent operator will be sure to take a backup of the database for each OpenStack project. Since most OpenStack services make heavy use of the database to persist things such as states and metadata, a corruption or loss of data could render your OpenStack cloud unusable. Current database backups can help rescue you from this fate. MySQL users can use the `mysqldump` utility to take a back up of all OpenStack databases:

```
mysqldump --opt --all-databases > all_openstack_dbs.sql
```

Similarly, Postgres users can take a back up of all OpenStack databases with a command similar to the one shown here:

```
pg_dumpall > all_openstack_dbs.sql
```

Your cadence for backups will depend on your environment and tolerance for data corruption or loss. You should store these backups in a safe place and occasionally deploy test restores from the data to ensure that they are working as expected.

Monitoring

Monitoring is often your early warning system that something is going wrong in your cluster. Your monitoring system can also be a rich source of information when it there comes a time to troubleshoot issues with the cluster. There are multiple options available to monitor OpenStack. Many of your current application monitoring platforms will handle OpenStack just as well as any other Linux system. Regardless of the tool you select to do your monitoring, there are several parts of OpenStack you should focus on.

Resource monitoring

OpenStack is typically deployed on a series of Linux servers. Monitoring the resources on those servers is essential. A set-it-and-forget-it attitude is a recipe for disaster. Things you may want to monitor on your host servers include the following:

- A CPU
- A disk
- Memory
- The log file size
- Network I/O
- A database
- A message broker

OpenStack quotas

OpenStack operators have the option of setting usage quotas for each tenant/project. As an administrator, it is helpful to monitor a project's amount of usage, as it pertains to these quotas. Once users reach a quota, they may not be able to deploy additional resources. Users may misinterpret this as an error in the system and report it to you as such. By keeping an eye on the quotas, you can proactively warn users as they reach their thresholds or you can decide to increase the quotas as appropriate. Some of the services have client commands that can be used to retrieve quota statistics. As an example, take a look at the `nova absolute-limits` command here:

```
nova absolute-limits
```

```
+---------------------+------+-------+
| Name                | Used | Max   |
+---------------------+------+-------+
| Cores               | 1    | 20    |
| FloatingIps         | 0    | 10    |
| ImageMeta           | -    | 128   |
| Instances           | 1    | 10    |
| Keypairs            | -    | 100   |
| Personality         | -    | 5     |
| Personality Size    | -    | 10240 |
| RAM                 | 512  | 51200 |
| SecurityGroupRules  | -    | 20    |
| SecurityGroups      | 1    | 10    |
| Server Meta         | -    | 128   |
| ServerGroupMembers  | -    | 10    |
| ServerGroups        | 0    | 10    |
+---------------------+------+-------+
```

The `absolute-limits` command in Nova is nice because it displays the project's current usage along with the quota maximum, making it easy to note that a project/tenant is close to the limit.

RabbitMQ

RabbitMQ is the default message broker used in OpenStack installations. However, if it is installed as is out the box, it can become a single point of failure. Administrators should consider clustering RabbitMQ and activating mirrored queues.

Clustering

You can confirm whether or not your RabbitMQ installation is operating as a cluster by running the `cluster status` command:

```
rabbitmqctl cluster_status
Cluster status of node 'rabbit@tc-ost1' ...
[{nodes,[{disc,['rabbit@tc-ost1']}]},
 {running_nodes,['rabbit@tc-ost1']},
 {partitions,[]}]
...done.
```

In the preceding output, note that in the `running_nodes` section, there is only one node listed. This is an indication that we are not running clustered RabbitMQ. For details on how to cluster RabbitMQ, refer to the latest Rabbit documentation at `https://www.rabbitmq.com/clustering.html`.

Mirrored queues

In addition to clustering Rabbit, you should also consider using mirrored queues. OpenStack leverages RabbitMQ queues, and by default, queues in Rabbit are located on a single node even if you are running a Rabbit cluster. Since the queue remains on one node by default, if you lose that node, you will lose the messages in that queue. The answer to this problem is to leverage mirrored queues. When enabled, these queues will be mirrored across multiple nodes. If the master node goes down for some reason, one of the node mirrors can take over for that queue.

To set up mirrored queues, make sure you are running RabbitMQ in a cluster mode. Once your cluster is set up, you need to set the high-availability policy for all non autogenerated queues. The following command will accomplish this:

```
rabbitmqctl set_policy ha-all '^(?!amq\.).*' '{"ha-mode": "all"}'
```

Once the policy has been set, you will need to configure each OpenStack service to leverage mirrored, high-availability queues. Locate the Rabbit section in the configuration file for each service and include the following values:

```
rabbit_hosts=rabbit1:5672,rabbit2:5672
rabbit_durable_queues=true
rabbit_ha_queues=true
```

More information about mirrored queues can be found in the Rabbit HA guide located at `https://www.rabbitmq.com/ha.html`.

Services

As we saw throughout this book, OpenStack deployments run multiple services. Each service typically runs multiple Linux processes. If you find yourself troubleshooting OpenStack, you should always make sure that the expected services are up and running. This is the equivalent of making sure that everything is *plugged* in. Monitoring the Linux processes for each service may save you a ton of headaches when it comes to troubleshooting.

Monitoring service processes

You should consider monitoring the key processes for each service. This could be as simple as configuring your monitoring service to run `ps --aux` on the service at regular intervals to ensure that the process is alive. Another option is to use a monitoring library that supports process monitoring and the ability to automatically restart services if they crash. Deploying methods that allow monitoring and automatic recovery of the OpenStack processes will save you time and headaches as you troubleshoot.

Backing up services

To assist in disaster recovery, administrators will want to take a backup of the critical files for each OpenStack service, along with the database. For details on how to take a backup of the database, refer to the section earlier in this chapter. To take a backup of the critical files for each service, you will need to look into three particular directories for each service. The directories you want to consider include the following:

*   `/etc/<project>`
*   `/var/lib/<project>`
*   `/var/log/<project>`

For example, to take a backup of the Glance image service, you would consider taking a backup of the files located at `/etc/glance`, `/var/lib/glance` and `/var/log/glance`.

Community resources

The OpenStack community is large, smart, and welcoming. If you find yourself stuck, the community will be willing and able to lend a hand. Don't hesitate to reach out for help if you find yourself hitting a dead end. The community provides a variety of tools and resources that can help you with troubleshooting.

Testing

The OpenStack software comes with an extensive suite of tests that are used during the development process to ensure a high-level of quality. This test suite can also be useful to the troubleshooter as a means to keep an eye on the overall reliability of your installation. This test suite can help you ensure that the software is running as intended. You can run the suite periodically against the various projects you are using and check for any errors. Not every error will need to be addressed, but this information could lead to early clues pointing to potential trouble in your stack.

Bugs

There are times when you are troubleshooting and you just hit a wall. You may try each of the techniques discussed in this book, but still find yourself stuck. Do not forget that OpenStack is an active project and is constantly under development. While the community works extremely hard to make and keep the software as reliable as possible, there are times when bugs slip through. If you run across an issue you cannot resolve, you may want to check for any bug reports similar to what you are experiencing. OpenStack bugs are tracked at `http://bugs.launchpad.net/openstack`. In addition, if you think you may have discovered a new bug that has not been reported, you can use this site to file bug reports.

Ask.openstack.org

The `Ask.openstack.org` website is where you can go to ask questions about OpenStack. It is also helpful to browse through answers given by other community members. This site is an excellent tool to leverage when you need help with the software and your deployment in general. This site is curated by volunteers from the OpenStack community, who are there to help when you get stuck. If you happen to come across a question that you know the answer to, I'd encourage you to provide your answer. This is an easy way for you to give back to the community.

Summary

OpenStack is leading open source software that is used to run private clouds. Its popularity has grown exponentially since it was founded by Rackspace and NASA. The output of this engaged community is staggering, resulting in plenty of new features finding their way into OpenStack with each release. The project is at a size now where no one can truly know the details of each service. When working with such a complex project, it is inevitable that you are going to run into problems, bugs, errors, issues, and plain old trouble. Our goal with this book was to give you the tools necessary to tackle those problems and find your path to a solution. We hope this book helps you get unstuck and start stacking.

Index

M

message broker tools
about 15
RabbitMQ 15-17
meter list command
about 130, 131
Glance meters 131
Nova meters 131, 132
methodologies
defining, with OpenStack 7
MySQL
Mytop 137
Percona Toolkit 138
SHOW STATUS statement 136
Mytop
about 137
header section 137
thread section 138

N

networking problems, OpenStack cluster
about 56
active instance, ping issue 56
IP address, missing 60-62
network namespaces 58-60
security groups, using 56-58
Neutron
about 53
issues, identifying 53
logs 55
services and agents 54, 55
troubleshooting tools 63
using, with Nova 89, 90
Neutron client 65
Neutron logs 55
Nova
about 67
services, checking 67
supporting services 79
using, with Glance 88, 89
using, with Neutron 89, 90

Nova API service (nova-api service)
about 68, 69
address, already in use 70
permission error 70
Nova authentication
about 83
correct service endpoints, checking 87, 88
Keystone, setup 83
service user, setting up 84-87
Nova compute service
(nova-compute) 75-77
Nova conductor service
(nova-conductor) 77-79
Nova scheduler service
(nova-scheduler) 71-74

O

OpenStack
about 1, 2
advantages 1
Barbican 5
bugs, URL 144
Ceilometer 4
Cinder 4
Congress 6
defining 2
Designate 6
documentation 5
Glance 3
Heat 4
Horizon 4
Ironic 5
Keystone 3
Magnum 5
Neutron 3
Nova 3
Oslo 4
Swift 4
troubleshooting methodology and tools 7
Trove 5
OpenStack Client
checking 23
client debug mode 23

CPSIA information can be obtained
at www.ICGtesting.com
Printed in the USA
FSOW04n2334300316
18643FS